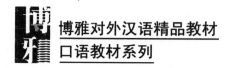

博雅对外汉语精品教材
口语教材系列

初级汉语口语（提高篇）

（第三版）

ELEMENTARY SPOKEN CHINESE (Improvement)
（Third Edition）

课文与练习

戴桂芙　刘立新　李海燕　编著

北京大学出版社
PEKING UNIVERSITY PRESS

图书在版编目 (CIP) 数据

初级汉语口语 . 提高篇 / 戴桂芙，刘立新，李海燕编著 . —3 版 . —北京：北京大学出版社，2015.1
（博雅对外汉语精品教材）
ISBN 978-7-301-25388-5

Ⅰ.①初… Ⅱ.①戴… ②刘… ③李… Ⅲ.①汉语—口语—对外汉语教学—教材 Ⅳ.① H195.4

中国版本图书馆 CIP 数据核字 (2015) 第 018009 号

书　　　名	初级汉语口语（提高篇）（第三版）
著作责任者	戴桂芙　刘立新　李海燕　编著
责 任 编 辑	刘　正　沈浦娜
标 准 书 号	ISBN 978-7-301-25388-5
出 版 发 行	北京大学出版社
地　　　址	北京市海淀区成府路 205 号　100871
网　　　址	http://www.pup.cn　新浪微博：@ 北京大学出版社
电 子 信 箱	zpup@ pup.cn
电　　　话	邮购部 62752015　发行部 62750672　编辑部 62753334
印 刷 者	三河市博文印刷有限公司
经 销 者	新华书店

889 毫米 ×1194 毫米　大 16 开本　15.5 印张　295 千字
1997 年 10 月第 1 版
2004 年 9 月第 2 版
2015 年 1 月第 3 版　2018 年 3 月第 3 次印刷

定　　　价　72.00 元（全二册、附 1 张 MP3 光盘）

第三版改版说明

　　这是一套经典汉语口语教材，自1996年出版以来，受到国内外汉语学习者和汉语教师的广泛好评，先后两次改版，数十次印刷，至今畅销不衰。

　　本套教材分初、中、高三个级别，每级分1、2和提高篇三册。每课分为课文、注释、语言点和练习等部分。每三至五课为一个单元，每单元附有口语常用语、口语知识及交际文化知识等。

　　本套教材从零起点起，初级前三课为语音集中教学阶段，后续课程根据情景和功能灵活设课，循序渐进，急用先学，即学即用。教材的选词范围主要以《汉语水平词汇与汉字等级大纲》为参照，初级以甲、乙级词为主，学习初级口语常用句式、简单对话和成段表达；中级以乙、丙级词为主，以若干主线人物贯串始终，赋予人物一定的性格特征和语言风格；高级以丁级词为主，第1、2册以一个典型的中国家庭为主线，以类似剧本的形式展开故事情节，展示中国家庭和社会的多个侧面。

　　本套教材的主要特点是：

　　1. 与日常生活紧密结合，学以致用；

　　2. 语言点解释简单明了，通俗易懂；

　　3. 练习注重结构与交际，丰富实用。

　　本套教材每个级别可供常规汉语进修生或本科生一学年之用，或供短期生根据实际水平及课时灵活选用。

　　第三版主要针对以下内容进行修订：

　　1. 对课文、例句及练习中过时的内容做了修改和替换，使之更具时代感；

　　2. 对少量语言点及解释做了调整和梳理，使之更加严谨，便于教学；

　　3. 对部分练习做了增删，使之更具有针对性和实用性。

北京大学出版社汉语及语言学编辑部

2014 年 3 月

序

随着改革开放的深入发展，对外汉语教学也日益受到人们的重视。来华的留学生人数也在增加。这些留学生中，虽然也有要通过汉语学习中国文化的，但其中有不少是要利用汉语和中国通商或进行政治、外交等诸方面活动的。在这种情况下，口语能力就显得特别重要。许多留学生都希望在短期内学好一口流利的普通话以便进行工作。

我们的汉语口语教学起步较晚。五六十年代虽然已有不少国家的留学生，可以说都是要打好汉语基础再入系深造的。我们对口语会话能力并未给以特殊的重视。"文化大革命"以后，开始有些口语课本出现，这些口语课本都是在会话内容上强调要贴近留学生生活、要能介绍中国文化、要能教给留学生得体的汉语、要能引起学生兴趣，等等。

诚然，上述各方面对口语教材都是非常重要的。但是要提高口语教学质量、改善口语教材的编写，却是个更重要的问题。

1996年起戴桂芙同志和两位青年教师在教授初级口语的同时，边实践、边总结、边研究、边编写，写成了今天这部初级口语课本。在编写课文时，她们没有忘记课文要贴近学生生活、要介绍中国文化、要语言得体、活泼有趣等等。因为这是所有口语教师都十分注意的。我认为她们把过去以词语为单位的教学法改革为以句型为单位的教学法才是最重要而有意义的改革。

为什么要把句型本位作为口语教学的出发点？这种变动有什么道理？我认为教材离不开学生的特点。成人学习外语都是想短期速成、目标明确。在一定的语言环境下教给学生恰当的句型，叫他们会话，这是符合学生要求的，也是便于学生掌握的。这样的教学效果肯定会较好的。

因为有句型本位的训练，初级口语也能训练学生成段表达的能力。这也有利于培养学生用汉语进行思维的能力，从而为他们尽早掌握符合汉语习惯的口语创造条件。

戴桂芙、刘立新、李海燕三位同志善于深思、勇于创新，为口语教学开新路。我祝她们取得更大成绩，为对外汉语教学立新功！

邓 懿

1997 年 7 月

第三版前言

　　《初级汉语口语》（1、2和提高篇）第二版出版至今，已近10载，此间这套教材重印多次，作为编者，我们深感欣慰。然而，随着社会生活的变化，语言的发展，教学理念的更新，教材，尤其是语言教材有必要得到修订和完善。为此，在北京大学出版社和同行们的帮助下，我们广泛搜集了使用过这部教材的北京大学对外汉语教育学院以及其他高校老师们的意见，也参考了一些针对这套教材所进行的研究成果（学生毕业论文、学术会议论文），对教材再次进行了修订。

　　本次修订的原则是：去除个别硬伤；剔除过时的内容，更新语料；在保持原有精华内容的基础上，尽量保持各课容量的均衡，适当降低难度，以便与《中级汉语口语》（1、2和提高篇）更自然地衔接。具体说来，我们在以下方面做了修改：

　　1. 课文和练习：

　　更新了语料，删除了一些过时的内容。有的课文全部重写，如原第一册的第十三课题目"我去图书馆上网"改为"我去图书馆借书"，用网上购书和寄快递的内容替换了原来过时的话题；尽量将长句改为短句，使语言更加口语化、自然化；使课文题目与课文内容相吻合；课文前或课文中的情景说明尽量简单，第一、二册增加了英译；对一些练习降低了难度。

　　第二册每课练习中增加了一项"每课一句"，内容是体现中国文化的名言，以增强教材的趣味性。由于原来的提高篇内容较多，本次修订精简了两课，由原来的十八课改为十六课。提高篇话题主要为社会生活内容，人物表不再适用，因此删除。第一册和第二册课数不变。

　　2. 语言点注释：

　　增加了语言点注释索引；对于用法较多的语言点，只出当课中的用法，以减轻学生的学习负担；语言点数量每课尽量均衡，有的只在练习中出现，练会即可；减少了对于初级学生有难度的语言点项目；一些词语与语言点的选择尽量考虑到语块因素，如"怎么了"。

　　3. 生词：

　　尽量增加生词在课文和练习中的重现率，减少了补充词语和难词；对于多义词语或句式，只出当课中的义项，其他义项出现时再作为新词语出现，如"送快递""送朋友"的"送"；补充词语尽量在后面的课文中作为生词出现，而且每课数量尽量均衡。

4．插图：

删掉了一些与课文内容无关的插图，更新了过时的图片，补充了一些新图片，如快递单、高铁票等。

这次修订，是这套教材第二次修订，是我们又一次新的努力。非常感谢为此付出心血的北京大学出版社编辑沈岚女士、刘正先生，以及为这套教材提出修订意见的各位同行。非常感谢为第三版修订内容进行英文、日文和韩文翻译的萧大龙先生、薛菲女士、井冈千寻女士和刘在恩女士。我们期待修订后的教材能够继续受到教师和学生们的欢迎，并能为更多喜爱汉语的外国学生打好口语基础助一臂之力。

编　者

2014 年 2 月

Foreword to the Third Edition

The second edition of *Elementary Spoken Chinese (I, II and Improvement)* has been almost published for ten years so far, reprinted many times. As authors, we are really gratified. However, with the change of society, development of language, as well as innovation on teaching philosophy, textbooks, especially language teaching textbooks are required to be updated. With the help of Peking University Press and peers, we have conducted a large scale survey on this series of textbooks from teachers on Teaching Chinese as a Second Language, suggestions and academic research (including theses and conference papers on this series of textbooks) are used as reference. Then we have revised the second edition of *Elementary Spoken Chinese (I, II and Improvement)*.

The third edition is based on the following principles: to correct mistakes; to delete the out-of-date content and update the corpus; to keep balance of the content of each lesson and reduce difficulties for smoothly connecting with *Intermediated Spoken Chinese (I, II and Improvement)*. We revised as follows:

1. Texts and exercises:

The corpus has been updated, and out-of-date contents have been deleted. For example, lesson thirteen was changed from "I'm going to the library to surf the internet" to "I'm going to the library to borrow a book". To buy and deliver books on internet replaced the original, out-of-date topic.

Long sentences are revised to be shorter sentences, so as to make the language more colloquial and natural; topics are more identical to the content of the texts; the scene descriptions in the texts are more concise, English translation is accompanied with the scene descriptions. Difficulties of some exercises are reduced.

In *Elementary Spoken Chinese II*, "One sentence a day" is added, which are from quotations indicating Chinese culture, for appealing to the students. The third edition of *Elementary Spoken Chinese (Improvement)* was reduced two lessons, from eighteen lessons to sixteen lessons. Since *Improvement* is mainly about social life, so the character sheet is not necessary, which is deleted. lessons of *Elementary Spoken Chinese I and II* remain the same.

2. Language points:

The index of language points is added. The language points are precisely interpreted the exact usage in this lesson, for students to have a good command. The amount of language points in each lesson keeps with consistent, some only occur in the exercises. Some difficult language points were removed. Language chunks, for example, "怎么了" is included in the language points.

3. Vocabulary:

The frequency of recurrence of new words in the text and exercises is increased, and the supplementary and difficult words are reduced. For multiple meanings words or patterns, only the meaning used in this lesson is discussed. The other meanings will be presented as new words, for example, "送" in "送快递" and "送朋友"; Supplementary words are also presented as new words in the later texts, and the amount of each lesson keeps balance.

4. Illustrations:

Illustrations unrelated to the texts were deleted. Outdated illustrations have been updated. Some new pictures are provided, for example, express list, high-speed rail ticket, etc.

The third edition of *Elementary Spoken Chinese (I, II and Improvement)* is our new effort. Many thanks to the editors, Ms. Shen Lan and Mr. Liu Zheng, and those advice-giving peers. In addition, we would like to sincerely thank Mr. Xiao Dalong, Ms. Xue Fei, Ms. Ioka Chihiro and Ms. Liu Zai'en for their contribution to the English, Japanese, and Korean translations. We hope this series of revised textbooks continue to be welcomed, and be very helpful to those foreign students who love the Chinese language.

Authors
February, 2014

第二版前言

　　《初级汉语口语》（上、下）出版七年多来，一直是颇受欢迎的教材，已重印十次。国内及海外多所院校使用，得到广泛肯定与好评。现在改版后的《初级汉语口语》（1、2册和初级提高篇）正以全新的面貌迎接着它更多的使用者，我们衷心期待着大家的支持和指正。

　　改版的原因有这么三点：第一，为了进一步开掘教材的实用性、有效性和使用的广泛性；第二，紧跟对外汉语教学的发展形势，紧跟社会发展的趋势；第三，融入使用者们提出的中肯而宝贵的建议。我们对《初级汉语口语》（上、下）做了全面的修订。

　　改版的基本原则是：在遵循原来的编写原则的基础上，突出以人为本，以学习者为主体，从教学的需要出发，更好地进行教与学的互动。

　　本次改版主要涉及以下几个方面：

　　一、　分册：由原来的两册六十课改为三册六十三课。其中第一册二十五课，新增语音教学三课；第二册二十课；初级提高篇十八课。每册均能满足大约一百五十学时的教学需要，并可根据学习者的程度，以其中任何一册为学习的起点，方便教学。

　　二、　课文：

　　1. 删除由于社会生活的发展、变化而过时的话题。如：关于北京的小公共汽车的话题。删除个别不具普遍性的语言现象，如："豆包不是包子"之类。增加当前学生生活中不可缺少的上网、发邮件等话题。

　　2. 降低难度，突显坡度，以便更自然地与《中级汉语口语》衔接。删除一些语法难点，如一些副词的用法。更加突出汉语口语的特点，将个别的长句改为短句；将一些复杂句式、特殊句式改为简单的常用句式；减少反问句式等。

　　三、　词语：以《汉语水平词汇与汉字等级大纲》（简称《大纲》）为准绳，进一步提高甲级词和甲级汉字的出现率，使所出现的甲级词和甲级汉字占到《大纲》的97％以上；删除了个别在初级阶段学习难度较大的乙、丙级词，删除了个别较难理解的俗语、习用语和北京话词语。一些当前生活中的常用词如"电脑""手机"等，虽然《大纲》未收，因话题的需要增加进去；词语的重现率有较大提高；附录中增加了词语总表和量词表。

四、 注释：随着课文的改写和增删，个别条目也有所调整。正文力求更加简明、准确，例句降低难度，尽量使用已学过的话题和词语，减少生词和难句。

五、练习：注释过的语言现象，基本上都有练习。练习项目数量更多，形式也更生动活泼。每课练习一般不少于七项，有的多到十一二项。第一册自始至终贯穿语音和声调训练，除用所学词语外，还选用了绕口令和古代诗词，不但增加了文化色彩，而且也提高了训练的情趣。练习的参考答案附后。第二册和初级提高篇的练习，除继续进行一些简单模仿性的练习外，更多的是可自由表达和发挥的创造性练习、成段表达练习。初级提高篇每课最后增加了"说一说，笑一笑"，素材取自《健康文摘报》摘录的小笑话，根据教学需要加以改写，意在使学习者通过说笑，轻松愉快地训练口语表达能力。

六、 翻译：除英文翻译外，词语部分增加了日文翻译和韩文翻译。课文、词语、注释、练习和"你知道吗？"的英文都是重新翻译的。日文翻译为岩川明子女士，韩文翻译为郑珠丽女士，课文和词语部分英文翻译为徐浣女士，第二版前言、注释、练习和"你知道吗？"为段孟华女士。

七、 插图：所有插图全部是新作。课文中的插图生动、有美感。练习中的插图贴切，更有助于学习者理解题意，快速、完美地进行练习。

八、 录音：为保证质量，录制了 CD 盘。

九、 排版：新的体例、版式及双色印刷使改版后的课本从形式上也焕然一新，比第一版更加清晰、醒目。第一册各课与第二册每段课文同时编排汉字和拼音，初级提高篇中的课文全部只写汉字并标注口语的实际声调。

十、 装订：为了更方便学习、阅读和查找，每册课本和附录分装两册。课本册包括课文、注释、练习和"你知道吗？"；附录册包括每课生词、练习中的补充词语、词语总表、名词量词搭配表、课文的英文翻译等。

本次改版的分工：第一册由李海燕主笔；第二册由刘立新主笔；初级提高篇由戴桂芙主笔。改版原则、改版大纲、改版内容等均经三人多次研讨，并数易其稿。全稿由戴桂芙审定。

本次改版的成功，是作者们的精诚、默契、愉快的合作结果，同时也与各方面的支持和帮助分不开。在此我们衷心感谢北京大学对外汉语教育学院领导的支持；衷心感谢所有对《初级汉语口语》第一版提出过建议和意见的老师和学生，特别要感谢北京大学对外汉语教育学院的老师们；衷心感谢为本次改版的翻译工作付出心血的四位女士；感谢插图的各位作者；还要特别感谢北京大学出版社和责任编辑郭力、沈浦娜女士；感谢审阅第二版前言英语译文的沈岚女士；感谢所有为本次改版付出劳动的朋友们！

此时此刻，我们特别怀念曾为《初级汉语口语》（上、下）作序的邓懿先生。她鼓励我们："为口语教学开新路""为对外汉语教学立新功！"我们缅怀邓先生的最好行动就是：再接再厉，为实现她对我们的殷切期望不懈努力！

戴桂芙　刘立新　李海燕

2003 年 12 月于北京大学

9

Foreword to a Revised Edition

Elementary Spoken Chinese (*1, 2*) sold well for over seven years after publishing , and was reprinted ten times. The textbook earned a favorable comment in many universities both in China and foreign countries. Now the revised *Elementary Spoken Chinese* (*1, 2 and Improvement*) is meeting more readers with a brand-new look. Your suggestions are very much welcome.

The reasons for revision are as follows:

First, to make it more effective and applicable and can be used extensively. Second, with the development of teaching Chinese as a foreign language, it has to be kept updated. Third, the readers' pertinent and valuable suggestions are incorporated into the textbook. Thus, revision was made to the previous *Elementary spoken Chinese* (*1, 2*).

The principle of the revision is: based on the previous compiling principle, with emphasis on the individual, which is student-centered for meeting the needs of teaching and learning.

The revisions are as follows:

First, dividing volumes: the previous textbook of 60 lessons in two volumes is changed into 63 lessons in three volumes. There are 25 lessons in volume 1, with three Phonetics lessons added; there are 20 lessons in volume 2; there are 18 lessons in volume of elementary improvement. Every volume can meet the needs of 150 teaching hours. The learner can choose the volume that suits his/ her level.

Second, text:

1. The outdated topics are deleted due to the development of society. e. g. the topic of mini buses in Beijing. Some language phenomena that are not in extensive use are deleted as well, e.g. " 豆包不是包子 ", etc. Topics regarding students' daily life are added such as access to Internet and sending Emails, etc.

2. The degree of difficulty is decreased and the learning process can be advanced step by step for using *Intermediate Spoken Chinese* smoothly. Some difficult grammar points are deleted, e.g. usages of some adverbs. Some long sentences are changed into short ones; some complex or special

sentence patterns are changed into common ones, the rhetorical sentences are deleted for indicating the characteristics of Spoken Chinese.

Third, words: *Syllabus of Chinese Words and Characters* (Syllabus in short) is used as a criterion, the frequency of the first-degree words and characters is increased, which covers more than 97% of those words in the Syllabus. Several second or third degree words and characters are deleted, which are difficult for students of elementary Chinese level. Some sayings, idioms and words of Beijing dialect are deleted as well. Some commonly-used words in daily life such as "电脑" "手机" are added, although they are not collected in the Syllabus. The repetition rate of words is greatly increased; a general vocabulary list and a table of measure words are added in the appendix.

Fourth, notes: with revision of texts, several items are adjusted as well. The text is aimed to be more concise and accurate, and the difficulty of examples is lowered as well. The topics and words that the students have learnt before are used for avoiding new words and difficult sentences.

Fifth, exercises: the language phenomena that are explained are mostly accompanied with exercises. The exercises are diversified and vivid. There are no less than seven items on the exercises, sometimes eleven or twelve items. Phonetics and tone exercises are through the beginning to the end in volume 1; the new words, tongue twister and ancient poems are selected as well for students to know about the cultural context. The key to exercises is attached afterwards. There are more expression exercises, narrative exercises in paragraph and creative exercises in volume 2 and volume of elementary improvement, except the mimic exercises in volume 1. "Discuss and have fun" is added in volume of elementary improvement, which is extracted from *Health Digest Weekly*. According to the needs of teaching and learning, some changes are made for the learners to practice their speaking skills under a happy and easy language environment.

Sixth, translation: except the English translation, Japanese and Korean translations are added. The texts, words, notes, exercises and "Do you know?" are all retranslated. The Japanese translators is Ms. Yanchuan Mingzi. The Korean translator is Ms. Zheng Zhuli. The English translation of texts and words is Ms. Xu Huan, and the English translation of the preface, notes, exercises and "Do you know?" is Ms. Duan Menghua.

Seventh, iconography: all the iconographs are newly made. They are lively and aesthetic, which are helpful for students to understand and do the exercises quickly and properly.

Eighth, recording: to guarantee the quality, the CD is available.

Ninth, typeset: new layout, format and two-color printing technology make a new look of the revised edition, which are clearer and more marked. All the lessons in volume 1 and volume 2 are both Chinese characters and Pinyin. Texts in volume of elementary improvement are just Chinese characters, with tone-marks given as well.

Tenth, binding: For convenience of learning, reading and checking, the textbook and appendix are binding respectively. The textbook is consisted of texts, notes, exercises and "Do you know?". There are new words, complementary words of exercises, vocabulary, measure words and English translation of texts, etc. in the appendix.

The main author of volume 1 is Ms. Li Haiyan; Ms. Liu Lixin is the author of volume 2; and the volume of elementary improvement is Ms. Dai Guifu. The details of revision such as the principle, syllabus and content are discussed many times, and changes are made quite a lot. Ms. Dai Guifu has made the final revision.

The success of this revised edition is due to the authors' contributions; supports from other aspects are very much appreciated as well. Our heartfelt thanks are given to the leaders of International College for Chinese Language Studies of Peking University. Our thanks are also extended to teachers and students who have given their ideas to the previous *Elementary Spoken Chinese*, especially those teachers of International College for Chinese Language Studies of Peking University.

We are very grateful to translators, illustrators, and executive editors—Ms. Guo Li, Ms. Shen Puna and Ms. Shen Lan of this book. All the friends who are dedicated to this book are appreciated.

At this moment, Professor Deng Yi who has written the preface for this book is specially cherished. She encouraged us in the preface "Create a new approach of teaching Spoken Chinese", and "make new contributions to teach Chinese as a foreign language". The best way for us is to endeavor continuously and work harder for entertaining her expectations.

By Dai Guifu, Liu Lixin and Li Haiyan
December 2003 at Peking University

目 录
Contents

第 一 课　寒假过得很开心 ……………………………………………… 1

第 二 课　谁输谁赢还不一定呢！ ……………………………………… 9

第 三 课　麻烦您停一下儿车 …………………………………………… 16

第 四 课　我从小就不爱吃鱼 …………………………………………… 22

　　　　　你知道吗？（1）送礼的习惯 …………………………………31

第 五 课　看把你高兴的 ………………………………………………… 34

第 六 课　对不起，我来晚了 …………………………………………… 41

第 七 课　健康和快乐比什么都重要 …………………………………… 49

第 八 课　周末怎么过？ ………………………………………………… 57

　　　　　你知道吗？（2）热情与含蓄 ……………………………… 65

第 九 课　什么是真正的男女平等？ …………………………………… 67

第 十 课　我是来找工作的 ……………………………………………… 76

第十一课　请你参加我们的婚礼 ……………………………………… 84

第十二课　爱生活的人永远年轻 ……………………………………… 93

　　　　　你知道吗？（3）谦虚与礼让 ……………………………… 101

第十三课　我是个有口福的人 ………………………………………… 104

第十四课　城市好还是农村好？ ……………………………………… 112

第十五课　真为你高兴 ………………………………………………… 122

第十六课　为友谊干杯！ ……………………………………………… 130

　　　　　你知道吗？（4）节日与历法 ……………………………… 138

寒假过得很开心

Hánjià guò de hěn kāixīn

（第一天上课前）

老　　师：有几位新同学，欢迎你们！大家互相认识一下儿吧。

彼　　得：老师，我们已经认识了。

老　　师：是吗？给我介绍介绍。

彼　　得：这位同学是韩国人，叫金……，对不起，你的名字有点儿难记。

金云福：金云福，金银的"金"，白云的"云"，幸福的"福"。

彼　　得：对，对，金云福。（指另外一个同学）她是……

山田有美：我叫山田有美，日本人，请您多多关照！

老　　师：你们俩的名字都挺好听。下边谁接着说？

吴平春：我说。我是华裔，从美国来。我会说点儿广东话，不过，我想学普通话。

老　　师：你的名字？

吴平春：吴平春，口天"吴"，水平的"平"，春天的"春"。

金云福：（小声问彼得）咱们班怎么样？

彼　　得：别担心，咱们班同学可好了，老师也像朋友一样。

（在宿舍）

丽　　莎：我回来啦，安妮。

安　　妮：快把行李放下，我以为你回来得比我早呢。玩儿得一定很开心吧？

丽　莎：当然啦，可有意思了！

安　妮：我看看，你好像比以前瘦了，也黑了，不过更精神了。

丽　莎：别光说我了，你寒假过得怎么样？家里都好吧？

安　妮：都好，谢谢！对了，这是我家乡的特产，是我爸爸妈妈给你的。他
们还向你问好呢。

丽　莎：你父母真好！

安　妮：对了，昨天我碰见杰夫了。他说，你回来以后，大家聚聚。

（在聚会上）

彼　得：杰夫，好久不见了。你寒假回国了，还是旅行去了？

杰　夫：都不是，我哪儿也没去。

彼　得：那么长的假期，哪儿也没去？

杰　夫：你一定想不到，我去当英语老师了。

彼　得：你？当老师？

杰　夫：不信啊？学生们挺喜欢我的。

彼　得：感觉怎么样？

杰　夫：又辛苦又快乐。

金云福：彼得，哪位是王平呀？你老说他是个有意思的人，快给我介绍介绍
吧。

彼　得：看我，把这个忘了。走，我介绍你们认识认识。

（王平对朋友们说）

这个寒假我过得很开心。春节是我爷爷八十岁生日，我们全家都回老家了。在那儿过春节比在北京热闹多了。回到我小时候生活过的地方，也是我出生的地方，我感到特别亲切。老家的变化太大了，小时候的朋友们也都长成大人了，我都认不出他们来了。

注 释　Notes

1. 广东话和普通话

广东话是汉语方言的一种，也称粤（yuè）方言或粤语。普通话是现代汉语的标准语，以北京语音为标准音，以北方话为基础方言，以典范的现代白话文著作为语法规范。

"广东话"（Guangdong dialect）is one of the Chinese dialects, which can also be called "粤方言" or "粤语"(Cantonese). 普通话（Mandarin）is the common language in modern Chinese, which takes Beijing pronunciation as the standard pronunciation, the northern language as the basic dialect, and the model works in modern vernacular Chinese as grammatical standard.

2. 你老说他是个有意思的人

You always say that he's a funny guy.

"老"是副词，有"经常""一直""总是""很久"等意思。如：

The adverb "老" has the same meaning as "经常""一直""总是", and "很久". For example:

（1）周末他老（经常）去唱卡拉 OK。

（2）最近老（一直）没看电影了。

（3）这个冬天我老（总是）感冒。

（4）因为夜里老（很久）睡不着，所以上课的时候老（经常）没精神。

3. 我都认不出他们来了

I had a hard time recognizing them.

"出来"用在动词后，本义表示从里到外，这里表示对事物的辨别，比如"听出来、看出来、吃出来、尝出来"。"动词＋不＋出来"意思是无法辨别，宾语必须放在"出"和"来"之间。如：

"出来" is used after the verb, its original meaning is movement from inside to outside. Here it indicates a recognition of something, such as "听出来"(I can hear it/something), "看出来"（I can see it/something）, "吃出来""尝出来"(I can taste it/something). "Verb＋不＋出来" means unable to identify. The object have to be placed between "出" and "来". For example:

（1）我喝出来了，这是青岛啤酒。

（2）你看出我来了吗?

（3）我都听不出他的声音来了。

 练 习　Exercises

一 用正确的语调读句子 Read the following sentences in correct intonation

　　1. 大家互相认识一下儿吧。

　　2. 你的名字有点儿难记。

　　3. 咱们班同学可好了，老师也像朋友一样。

　　4. 我以为你回来得比我早呢。

　　5. 可有意思了！

　　6. 别光说我了，你寒假过得怎么样?

　　7. 那么长的假期，哪儿也没去?

　　8. 你? 当老师?

　　9. 我介绍你们认识认识。

　　10. 这个寒假我过得很开心。

二 根据课文的内容用自己的话回答问题

Answer the following questions in your own words according to the content of the text

1. 彼得的班上有几位新同学？请你介绍一下儿。
2. 丽莎寒假过得怎么样？
3. 安妮放假去旅行了吗？
4. 杰夫放假干什么了？感觉*怎么样？

三 请不看课文复述王平是怎么过这个寒假的，他的感觉怎么样

Please repeat without reading the text how Wang Ping spent the winter holidays and how his feeling was

四 仿照例句，用加点的词语完成并扩展句子

Following the examples, complete and extend the sentences by using the dotted words

1. 你的名字有点儿难记。→对不起，你的名字有点儿难记，请再说一遍。

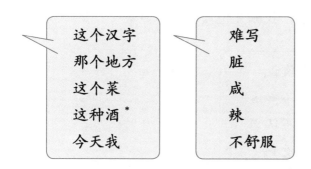

这个汉字
那个地方
这个菜
这种酒*
今天我

难写
脏
咸
辣
不舒服

2. 快把行李放下。→快把行李放下，咱们休息休息。

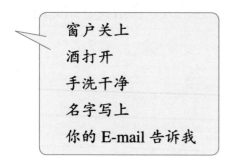

窗户关上
酒打开
手洗干净
名字写上
你的 E-mail 告诉我

3. 我以为你回来得比我早呢。→我以为你回来得比我早呢，原来你回来得比我晚。

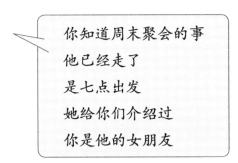

你知道周末聚会的事

他已经走了

是七点出发

她给你们介绍过

你是他的女朋友

4. 玩得一定很开心吧? → 你去了那么长时间，玩得一定很开心吧?

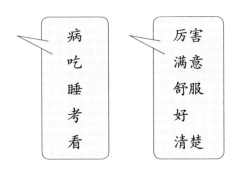

病　　厉害
吃　　满意
睡　　舒服
考　　好
看　　清楚

5. 我哪儿也没去。→星期天有事，我哪儿也没去。

我什么　　没说
我什么　　不知道
我谁　　　不认识
我哪个　　没买
我什么　　不喜欢

6. 快给我介绍介绍吧。→你老说他是个有意思的人，快给我介绍介绍吧。

来认识认识

给大家表演表演

去参观参观

关照关照他

跟我说说

7. 朋友们也都长成大人了。→朋友们也都长成大人了，我都认不出他们来了。

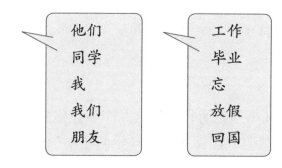

他们	工作
同学	毕业
我	忘
我们	放假
朋友	回国

五　根据图中提供的情况，两个人一组，通过问答了解图中的人

Two students make a group, talk about the persons in the picture by asking and answering questions, according to the information provided

张明，男，22岁，大学生，高个子，戴眼镜，还没有女朋友　　李文，女，25岁，山东人，护士*，长头发，很漂亮，男朋友姓王　　赵华，男，34岁，在电脑公司工作，结婚五年了，妻子是老师，儿子三岁　　白雪，女，56岁，律师，丈夫是医生，儿子和女儿都是大学生

六　读例句，用加点的词语完成对话

Read the examples and complete the dialogues by using the dotted words

1. 例：甲：咱们班怎么样？

　　　　乙：咱们班同学可好了，老师也像朋友一样。

　　（1）你住的地方怎么样？

　　（2）你最近生活怎么样？

　　（3）你的新同学怎么样？

2. 例：甲：小时候的朋友们变化大吗？

　　　　乙：变化太大了，我都认不出他们来了。

（1）告诉我你写的是什么？

（2）姐姐和妹妹长得太像了。

（3）你看，这是我小时候的照片。

七 谈一谈 Have a talk

1. 向同学们介绍你的汉语名字是哪几个字？为什么用这几个字做你的名字？

2. 你是老同学还是新同学？寒假（暑假）在哪儿过的？你们国家 * 的大学生在假期里常做什么？

3. 介绍一次难忘的假期生活。

4. 你的老家在哪儿？那儿怎么样？有什么特产？

5. 你知道中国人怎么过春节吗？

八 介绍介绍 Make an introduction

两个人一起互相介绍自己的情况 *，然后向全班介绍你的新同学。

九 说一说，笑一笑 Talk and laugh

缺点 *

老师：你认识到上课睡觉的缺点了吗？

学生：认识到了。

老师：缺点是什么？

学生：缺点是不如睡在床上舒服。

Defect

Teacher: Have you realized the shortcoming of sleeping in class?

Student: Yes, I've realized that.

Teacher: Then what's the shortcoming?

Student: It's not so comfortable as sleeping in bed!

Shuí shū shuí yíng hái bù yídìng ne!
谁 输 谁 赢 还 不 一 定 呢！

（在家里）

丈　夫：好球！加油！

妻　子：听，好像有人敲门。

丈　夫：快去看看。

邻　居：对不起，您家的电视能不能小点儿声？我母亲病了，需要安静……

妻　子：真对不起，影响你母亲休息了。

丈　夫：实在抱歉，我一看球就大喊大叫……

邻　居：咱们俩一样，都是球迷。现在几比几了？

（在校园里）

彼　得：走，看球去！

金云福：哪儿有球赛？

彼　得：学校足球场。

金云福：谁跟谁比？

彼　得：国际队对校队。

金云福：国际队？

彼　得：是啊，由外国留学生组成的队。他们踢得挺好的。

金云福：能赢校队吗？

彼　得：国际队也挺厉害的，谁输谁赢还不一定呢。

（在足球场上）

金云福：比赛开始了。

彼　得：国际队，加油！

金云福：七号摔倒了！快爬起来呀！

彼　得：没事儿，你看他挺轻松地就站起来了。

金云福：十三号怎么推人呢？

彼　得：裁判给了他一张黄牌儿。

金云福：罚得好！

彼　得：好球！进了！

（足球队长说）

　　我是国际足球队的队长，队员们都棒极了。一般每两周进行一次比赛，大家都很认真。我的女朋友是拉拉队的队长。有了他们的热情支持，比赛的时候，我们更有精神了，今天的比赛就是这样。开始的时候，大家很紧张，都怕输掉比赛。这时候，我听见了拉拉队员们的加油声："国际队一定赢！"离比赛结束还有最后一分钟的时候，我们队又踢进了一个球！2比1，我们队赢了！大家又是握手又是拥抱，高兴极了。

注　释　Notes

1. 国际队对校队

The international team against the school varsity team.

动词"对"在这里是"对阵"的意思，比喻相互竞争、比赛，是体育竞赛中的常用语。

Here the verb "对" means "to clash/encounter", and expresses mutual rivalry, competition. It is a commonly used term in athletic contests.

2. 由外国留学生组成的队

the team made up of the foreign students

"由……组成"是个固定格式，介词"由"跟它后边的名词一起构成介宾短语做"组成"的状语。如：

"由……组成" is a fixed pattern, the preposition "由" and its following noun is used as an adverbial of "组成". For example:

（1）我们班由几个国家的学生组成。
（2）由球迷组成的拉拉队很热情。

3. 黄牌儿

黄色的牌子。体育比赛中，运动员、教练员等严重犯规，裁判员出示黄牌儿给以警告。

Yellow card. If in the sports game, a player or a coach seriously breaks the rule, the judge will show a yellow card to give a warning.

4. 拉拉队

cheerleading squad

体育运动比赛时，在旁边给运动员呐喊助威的人。

The group of people on the side shouting and cheering for the athletes in the sports matches.

练 习 Exercises

一 用正确的语调读句子 Read the following sentences in correct intonation

1. 谁输谁赢还不一定呢。
2. 听，好像有人敲门。
3. 真对不起！
4. 实在抱歉！
5. 现在几比几了？
6. 谁跟谁比？
7. 国际队，加油！
8. 好球！进了！
9. 一定赢！

二 替换句中画线部分的词语 Substitute the underlined words in the sentences

1. 谁输　　　　　　谁赢　　　　　　还不一定呢。

是哥哥	是弟弟	我们谁也分不清楚
水平高	水平低	让他们比一比就知道了
学得好	学得差	他们的老师最了解了
该罚	不该罚	都得听裁判的
回答对了	回答错了	同学们都听得出来

2. 实在抱歉，我一看球就大喊大叫……

- 我忘了告诉你
- 我又迟到了
- 您的车我还没修好
- 我的手机没电了
- 影响您休息了

3. 咱们俩　　　　　　　　一样，都是　　　　　球迷。

> 女儿和妈妈
> 儿子和爸爸
> 我和你
> 我们大学和北大
> 妻子和丈夫

> 大夫
> 工程师
> 影迷
> 有名的大学
> 老师

4. 国际队　　　　　　　　　　是由　　　　　外国留学生组成的。

> 我们班
> 这个大学
> 那个大公司
> "你、好、吗"这几个汉字
> 中国

> 五个国家的学生
> 二十几个系
> 几个小公司
> 左右两部分
> 五十六个民族*

5. 一般每两周进行一次比赛。

> 一个月有一次考试
> 一个学期回一次家
> 每两个星期聚一聚
> 每隔三分钟来一辆车
> 下午玩一会儿

三　读一读，体会各句中"对"的不同意义

Read the sentences and learn the different meaning of " 对 " in each sentence

1. 你说得对。
2. 国际队对校队。
3. 他们是一对好夫妻*。
4. 朋友们对我都很好。
5. 足球队长对球迷说："队员们都棒极了。"

四　熟读课文，并快速完成下面的段落

Learn the text by heart and quickly complete the following paragraph

　　我是国际足球队的队长，队员们都（　　　　）极了。（　　　　　）每两周进行一次比赛，大家都很（　　　　）。我的女朋友是拉拉队的队长。有了他们的（　　　　　）支持，比赛的时候，我们（　　　　）更有精神了，今天的比赛就是这样。开始的时候（　　　　　），大家都很（　　　　）。这时候，我听见了拉拉队员们的加油声："国际队一定赢！"比赛快要（　　　）的时候，我们（　　　　）踢进了一个球！我们队（　　　　）了！大家又是（　　　）又是（　　　　），（　　　　）极了。

五　以拉拉队队长的身份说说国际队对校队比赛的情况

Describe the match between the international team and the school team supposing you are head of the cheerleading squad

六　根据情景设计对话　Make dialogues according to the situation

1. 一个球迷没买到票，请求门卫*让他进去看球。
2. 比赛后，一个队员向被自己不小心踢伤的队员道歉。
3. 一位老人告诉踢球的孩子注意安全。

七　介绍一场你印象深刻的球赛　Describe a match that deeply impressed you

参考词语和句式　Words and sentence patterns for reference

A 对 B	A 比 B	输	赢	由……组成	摔倒
落后	紧张	终于	推人	罚	

八　说一说，笑一笑　Talk and laugh

足球知识

球迷甲：足球比赛我看得多啦，我懂得足球方面的一切*知识*。

球迷乙：是吗？那你告诉我，足球网*有多少个网眼儿*？

Knowledge about football

Fan A: I've watched so many football games and I know all about football.

Fan B: Really? Then tell me how many holes are there on a football net?

没人合作 *

老师：你考试怎么不像你踢足球那么棒呢？

学生：老师，踢足球时有人合作，可考试时没人合作啊！

Nobody to cooperate with

Teacher: Why aren't you so good at taking exams as you playing football?

Student: Well, when I play football there are other members cooperating with me, but there isn't anybody to cooperate with in an exam!

Máfan nín tíng yíxiàr chē
麻烦您停一下儿车

（在公共汽车上）

乘　客：师傅，这车到动物园吗？

售票员：您坐反了，动物园在南边，这车是往北边开的。下了车，到马路对面坐车。

乘　客：劳驾，麻烦您停一下儿车。

售票员：不行，不到站不准停车。

乘　客：我坐错车了，快让我下去吧！

售票员：对不起，不是我不想帮您，马路上不能随便停车。

（出租车司机回家晚了）

妻　子：怎么这么晚才回来？

丈　夫：今天真倒霉，被罚了。

妻　子：什么？出什么事了？

丈　夫：不小心闯红灯了。

妻　子：没伤着人吧？

丈　夫：没有。

妻　子：以后小心点儿吧。你应该好好儿记住："高高兴兴上班去，平平安安回家来。"好让我们每天都放心哪。

丈　夫：以后，我一定要注意遵守交通规则，好让你们放心。

（交通新闻）

　　今天下午，本市又发生了一起交通事故。一个汽车司机酒后开车，闯了红灯，撞上了一辆从南往北开的公共汽车，结果一人重伤，两人轻伤。请司机师傅们一定要注意交通安全，不要酒后开车，更不要闯红灯，那太危险了。

注　释　Notes

1. 劳驾

Excuse me.

客套话。用于请别人做事或让路。中间可以加入被请的人。如：

Polite language.　Used to ask other people to do something or let one pass.　The title of the person being addressed/asked can be inserted into the sentence. For example:

（1）劳驾，请帮我开开门。

（2）劳您驾，请让我过去。

2. 不到站不准停车

The bus is not allowed to stop anywhere except bus stations.

这句话中用"不"做两次否定，实际上表示肯定，意思是"到了站才准许停车"。如：

In this sentence, twice negation of "不" in fact indicates affirmation. It means "the bus can only stop at the station". For example:

（1）这个公园，不买票不能进去。

（2）谁不遵守交通规则都不行。

3. 高高兴兴上班去，平平安安回家来

Go to work happily, return home safely!

这是在大街上的一句标语口号，用以提醒司机、行人在开车、乘车、骑车、走路时，都要遵守交通规则，注意安全，避免意外事故发生。

This is a slogan appearing on the streets, which is used to warn drivers and pedestrians that when driving, riding, and walking, we all need to obey traffic regulations and pay attention to security for avoiding accidents.

4. 高高兴兴上班去，平平安安回家来

"高高兴兴"和"平平安安"是双音节形容词"高兴"和"平安"的重叠。"AABB"式是双音节形容词重叠式的一种，如"热热闹闹""安安静静""辛辛苦苦"等。

"高高兴兴"and"平平安安"are reduplication of the two-syllable adjectives "高兴" and "平安". The pattern "AABB" is one of the reduplicating forms of disyllable adjectives, for example, "热热闹闹""安安静静""辛辛苦苦", etc.

5. 好让我们每天都放心哪

It'll let us feel relieved every day.

这里的"好"是助动词，意思是"可以、以便"，用于后一小句，表示前一小句中动作的目的。如：

The "好" here is a auxiliary verb which means "can" and so that. When used in the later clause, it indicates the purpose of the action in the previous clause. For example:

（1）告诉我你的电话号码吧，有事好给你打电话。

（2）甲：这么早你就要睡觉了？

　　　乙：晚上早点儿睡，明天早上好早点儿起床。

练 • 习 Exercises

一 用正确的语调读句子 Read the following sentences in correct intonation

1. 劳驾，麻烦您停一下儿车。
2. 我坐错车了，快让我下去吧！
3. 对不起，不是我不想帮您。
4. 怎么这么晚才回来？
5. 什么？出什么事了？
6. 高高兴兴上班去，平平安安回家来。
7. 不要酒后开车，更不要闯红灯。
8. 那太危险了。

二 根据课文内容用自己的话回答问题

Answer the following questions in your own words according to the content of the text

1. 那位乘客为什么不到站就要下车？
2. 为什么那辆公共汽车不能停车？
3. 那位出租车司机为什么回家晚了？他有什么倒霉事？
4. 那辆汽车为什么跟公共汽车撞上了？

三 替换句中画线部分的词语 Substitute the underlined words in the following sentences

1. 劳驾，麻烦您停一下儿车。

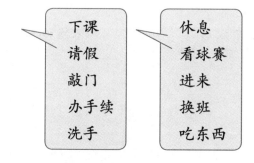

让一让，我要下车
帮我换点儿零钱*
开一下儿门
把窗户关上
能不能快点儿？

2. 不到站不准停车。

下课　　　休息
请假　　　看球赛
敲门　　　进来
办手续　　换班
洗手　　　吃东西

3. <u>对不起</u>，不是<u>我</u>　不<u>想帮你</u>。

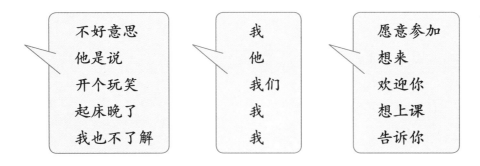

不好意思	我	愿意参加
他是说	他	想来
开个玩笑	我们	欢迎你
起床晚了	我	想上课
我也不了解	我	告诉你

4. <u>你应该好好儿记住</u>："高高兴兴上班去，平平安安回家来。"

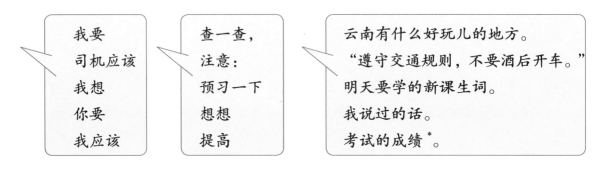

我要	查一查，	云南有什么好玩儿的地方。
司机应该	注意：	"遵守交通规则，不要酒后开车。"
我想	预习一下	明天要学的新课生词。
你要	想想	我说过的话。
我应该	提高	考试的成绩*。

5. <u>以后小心点儿吧</u>，<u>好让我们每天都放心哪</u>。

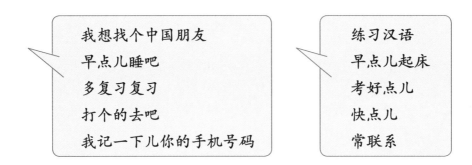

我想找个中国朋友	练习汉语
早点儿睡吧	早点儿起床
多复习复习	考好点儿
打个的去吧	快点儿
我记一下儿你的手机号码	常联系

四　用自己的话说一说课文中那条交通新闻的内容

Describe the content of the traffic news in the text in your own words

五　用提示的词语改说课文中的对话

Reorganize the dialogues in the text by using the given words

1. 坐公共汽车的乘客说：

　　参考词语：| 昨天　　去动物园　　上车以后　　坐反了　　不准停车 |

2. 开出租车的丈夫对妻子说：

　　参考词语：| 今天倒霉　　被　　伤人　　闯红灯　　以后注意　　罚　　好让 |

六 谈一谈 Have a talk

1. 你经常坐公共汽车吗？你喜欢坐公共汽车，还是骑自行车？为什么？

2. 公共汽车、出租车等上车、下车、停车都有什么不同？

3. 你被交通警察罚过吗？为什么被罚？

4. 你知道中国有哪些交通规则？和你的国家一样吗？有哪些不同？

5. 你看见过交通事故吗？当时的情况怎么样？

七 说一说，笑一笑 Talk and laugh

该说"谢谢"

奶奶*看见孙子*在家里的地上到处*爬，衣服脏得要命。她生气地对孙子说："你看你，把地都擦*干净了，你叫我说你什么好呢？"孙子说："奶奶，那您就该对我说：'谢谢！'"

You should say "thank you"

The grandma saw her grandson crawl around on the floor, making the clothes very dirty. She said angrily, "look at you, you have already wiped the floor with your clothes! What should I say to you?" The grandson answered, "well, grandma, you should say 'thanks' to me!"

Wǒ cóng xiǎo jiù bú ài chī yú

我从小就不爱吃鱼

（在餐厅里）

甲：快说，咱们吃什么？服务员等着呢。

乙：来个尖椒牛肉吧。

甲：好，辣的，我爱吃。我想要个炒蘑菇。

丙：再来个鱼吧。

甲：我从小就不爱吃鱼。不论怎么做，我都不爱吃。

丙：这儿的鱼不错，尝一次，也许你就爱吃了。

乙：来一个吧。鱼的营养丰富，都说吃鱼能让人聪明。

甲：现在吃，还来得及吗？好吧，陪你们吃，来一个就来一个吧。

丙：三个菜，够了，再来三杯可乐。主食要什么？

甲：一人一碗米饭吧。

乙：我现在又渴又饿。服务员，麻烦您快点儿行吗？

（杰夫和王平聊天儿）

杰 夫：中国的民族多，历史长，传统节日、民族节日是不是也多？

王 平：是啊，明天就是一个节日。

杰 夫：什么节？

王 平：端午节，翻译成英文叫"龙船节"。

杰　夫：放假吗？

王　平：放。那天家家都吃粽子，有的地方还举行划龙船比赛，挺有意思的。

杰　夫：什么是粽子？

王　平：粽子嘛，……这样吧，我奶奶年年都包，明天你去我家，咱们一起包，
　　　　一起吃。

（在王平家）

奶　奶：粽子煮好了，大家都来尝尝吧！

杰　夫：我从来没吃过粽子，真好吃！

王　平：好吃也得少吃点儿，还有好多菜呢。

杰　夫：刚才咱们都在包粽子，是谁做了这么多菜？

王　平：是我叫的外卖。

杰　夫：叫外卖？好办法！

王　平：哪天你没时间去食堂排队的话，也可以叫个外卖，又快又方便。

奶　奶：王平，别说了，快请客人多吃点儿吧！

（杰夫说）

　　校门外有一家小饭馆，是不久以前新开的。有一天，我散步时，路过这家饭馆，发现门口挂着一个牌子，上面写得很有意思："如果您吃得满意，请对朋友说；如果您吃得不满意，请对老板说。"我就进去点了一菜一汤，不但味道好得很，而且价钱十分便宜，服务也挺周到的。后来我又去过很多次，回回满意。老板都知道我爱吃什么了，他还说，回国后，我一定会想念他的饭馆。

注　释　Notes

1. 不论怎么做，我都不爱吃

No matter how it's made, I just don't like eating it.

"不论"，连词，表示条件或情况不同而结果不变，后边往往有并列的词语或表示任指的疑问代词等，下文多用"都""也""总是"等跟它呼应。如：

The conjunction "不论" indicates the unchanged result under different condition or situation, which is often followed by paratactic words or interrogative pronouns expressing indefiniteness, etc, with "都""也""总是" working in concert with in the later context. For instance:

（1）你不论什么时候来，我都欢迎。

（2）不论那个公司给我多少钱，我也不愿意去那儿工作。

（3）不论是学习还是工作，他总是认认真真的。

2. 来一个就来一个吧

If you want to get one, then just do so.

这句话表示同意对方提出的做某事的要求。口语中，常用"A 就 A 吧"这个格式来表示为满足对方要求而同意做某事。如：

This sentence expresses an agreement to the request of the other party in regard to doing something. The pattern "A 就 A 吧" is often used in spoken Chinese to express the agreement to doing sth. in order to satisfy the other party's request. For example:

（1）甲：对不起，我不想去了。

　　乙：不去就不去吧。

（2）甲：我不想吃馒头了，吃饺子好吗？

　　乙：吃饺子就吃饺子吧。

3. 端午节和粽子

Dragon Boat Festival and zongzi

"端午节"即"端五节"，又称"端节"，是中国的民族传统节日之一。时间在农历五月初五。相传古代诗人屈原在这一天投江自杀，后人为了纪念他，把这天当做节日。有吃粽子、赛龙船的风俗。

"粽子"是一种食品，用竹叶或苇叶把糯米等包住，扎成三角锥体或其他形状，煮熟后食用。

"端午节" and "端五节", also called "端节", is one of the traditional Chinese nationality holidays. It takes place on the 5th day of the 5th month of the lunar calendar. According to legend, the ancient poet Qu Yuan threw himself into a river and committed suicide on this day. In order to memorize him, later generations made this day a holiday. It has the traditions of eating zongzi and racing dragon boats.

"Zongzi" is a kind of food, using bamboo leaves or reed leaves to wrap polished glutinous rice and other things, bundled up into a triangular pyramid or in other shapes. It can be eaten after cooked.

4. 家家都吃粽子／回回满意

Every family eats zongzi; satisfied every time.

"家家"读作"jiājiā"，"回回"读作"huíhuí"（第二个"家""回"不能读成轻声）。量词的重叠。"家家"意思是"每家"，"回回"意思是"每回"即"每次"。其他常用的量词重叠形式还有："个个""场场""人人"等。

"家家" is read as "jiājiā", and "回回" is read as "huíhuí" (the second "jiā" and "huí" cannot be read in the neutral tone). In the reduplication of measure words, "家家"means"每家" (every family), "回回" means "每回" and "每次" (every time). Other commonly used reduplication of measure words are: "个个" "场场" "人人", etc.

5. 哪天你没时间去食堂排队的话，也可以叫个外卖。

> If you don't have time to line up at dining hall some day, you can order some take out.

助词"的话"用在表示假设的分句后边，引出下文。如：

Auxillary word "的话" is used at the end of a supposition sentence, to connect with the next clause in the sentence. For example:

（1）你喜欢的话，给你，我再买一个。

（2）不吃鱼的话，来个尖椒牛肉吧。

前边有"如果、要是"等呼应，假设的语气更重。如：

If in the front of the clause containing "的话" is "如果，要是", the tone of the supposition is stronger. For example:

（1）如果喝了酒的话，就不要开车了。

6. 不但味道好得很，而且价钱十分便宜。

> They tasted pretly good and the price was quite cheap too.

连词"不但"用在前一分句里，常跟后一分句中的"而且、并且"或"也、还、又"等搭配，"而且"等引出的意思更进了一层。如：

The conjunction "不但" is used in the front of the first clause of a sentence, and is often paired with the second clause's "而且，并且" or "也，还，又"."而且" denotes a further description. For example:

（1）我不但认识他，而且很了解他。

（2）鱼不但好吃，而且营养丰富。

7. 味道好得很

"得很"放在形容词后做程度补语，表示程度高。如：

"得很" is put after an adjective to form a degree complement, expressing a high degree. For example:

（1）交通方便得很。

（2）房间贵得很。

练 习　Exercises

一　用正确的语调读句子 Read the following sentences in correct intonation

1. 快说，咱们吃什么？

2. 我从小就不爱吃鱼。

3. 不论怎么做，我都不爱吃。

4. 现在吃，还来得及吗？

5. 好吧，陪你们吃，来一个就来一个吧。

6. 中国的民族多、历史长，传统节日、民族节日是不是也多？

7. 我从来没吃过粽子，真好吃！

8. 叫外卖？好办法！

9. 别说了，快让客人多吃点儿吧。

10. 不但味道好得很，而且价钱十分便宜。

二 替换句中画线部分的词语 Substitute the underlined words in the following sentences

1. 不论<u>怎么做</u>，<u>我</u> <u>都</u> <u>不爱吃</u>。

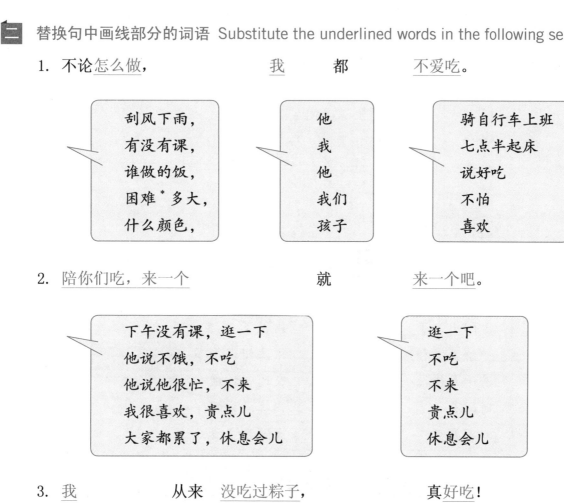

刮风下雨，
有没有课，
谁做的饭，
困难*多大，
什么颜色，

他
我
他
我们
孩子

骑自行车上班
七点半起床
说好吃
不怕
喜欢

2. <u>陪你们吃，来一个</u> <u>就</u> <u>来一个吧</u>。

下午没有课，逛一下
他说不饿，不吃
他说他很忙，不来
我很喜欢，贵点儿
大家都累了，休息会儿

逛一下
不吃
不来
贵点儿
休息会儿

3. <u>我</u> 从来 <u>没吃过粽子</u>， <u>真好吃</u>！

我
你
我
我
我

没走过这条路
没穿过这种衣服
见过这样的同屋
没碰见过这种事
没办过这样的事

远啊
漂亮
倒霉
生气
麻烦

4. <u>叫外卖</u>？好办法！

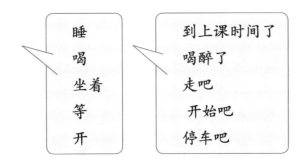

请老师参加
找中国朋友帮忙
一起包粽子
拿旧的换新的
现在先不告诉他

5. <u>别</u>说<u>了</u>，快<u>请</u>客人<u>多吃点儿吧</u>。

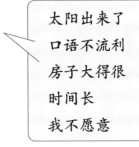

睡	到上课时间了
喝	喝醉了
坐着	走吧
等	开始吧
开	停车吧

6. <u>不但</u>味道<u>好得很</u>，　　　　<u>而且</u>价钱十分便宜。

太阳出来了
口语不流利
房子大得很
时间长
我不愿意

风停了
语法错误很多
交通挺方便
内容没意思
大家都不喜欢

7. <u>不但</u>味道<u>好</u>得很，<u>而且</u>价钱十分便宜。

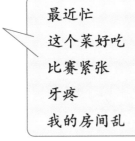

最近忙
这个菜好吃
比赛紧张
牙疼
我的房间乱

没时间出去玩儿
我回回都点一个
队员们都想赢不想输
什么东西也吃不了
别去我的房间了

8. 后来我又去过很多次，回回满意。

我打过好多次电话

我找过你几回

我经常在这儿吃饭

一个学期有三次考试

她参加聚会

没人接

你都不在

点这个菜

都考得不好

迟到

三　读例句，用加点的词语完成对话

Read the examples and complete the dialogues by using the dotted words

1. 例：甲：你爱吃鱼吗？

　　乙：我从小就不爱吃鱼，不论怎么做，我都不爱吃。

　（1）你每天都去锻炼身体吗？

　（2）你真的不相信我的话吗？

　（3）我想睡一会儿，什么地方比较安静？

2. 例：甲：中国的民族多、历史长，传统节日、民族节日是不是也多？

　　乙：是啊，明天就是一个节日。

　（1）你知道谁是他们班的汉语老师吗？

　（2）学校的医院是哪座楼？

　（3）哪天是你的生日？

3. 例：甲：今天下午六点下课，六点半有电影，没时间去食堂排队吃饭了。

　　乙：你没时间去食堂排队的话，就叫个外卖吧。

　（1）都十一点了，我还没复习完呢。

　（2）你身体不舒服，去医院找大夫看看吧。

　（3）快关门了，我还没选好要买的东西呢。

4. 例：甲：有时候十二点刚下课，十二点半又得上课，没时间去食堂排队吃饭。

　　乙：你没时间去食堂排队的话，也可以叫个外卖。

　（1）我不想花很多钱买新自行车，新车也容易丢。

　（2）同学们有问题要问老师，上课的时候没时间问怎么办？

　（3）明天去上海，六点就要起床，我怕起不来。

四 复述杰夫和那家小饭馆的故事，并仿照杰夫的话介绍一家你认为不错的饭馆

Repeat the story about Jeff and the small restaurant, then introduce to your classmates your favourate restaurant by imitating Jeff's words

五 谈一谈 Have a talk

1. 你爱吃鱼吗？你最爱吃什么菜？
2. 你吃过粽子吗？味道怎么样？
3. 你常去饭馆吃饭吗？有没有你满意的饭馆？
4. 说说你理想的饭馆是什么样的？
5. 你知道中国有哪些节日？
6. 你们国家有哪些节日？

六 食品*展 Food show

　　每个学生带来一种自己做的或你爱吃的或有你们国家特点的食品，先介绍这种食品的做法，然后请大家尝一尝。

　　Each student brings a kind of food which is cooked by yourself, or is your favorite, or is typical in your country. First introduce how the food is cooked and then invite others to have a taste.

七 开饭馆 Run a restaurant

　　如果你想开一家饭馆，自己当经理。你打算怎样当这个经理？把你的打算讲给同学们听。听了几个人的打算后，同学们可以向他们提出各种问题，然后讨论谁开的饭馆可能最受欢迎，为什么？

　　If you want to run a restaurant and work as the manager by yourself, then how will you make a manager? Tell your classmates about your plan. The class can raise all kinds of questions after they have listened to several plans, and then discuss whose restaurant will be the most popular one, and why?

八 说一说，笑一笑 Talk and laugh

十分容易

　　考试前，学生们紧张地问老师，考试难不难？老师只回答了一句："十分容易。"大家都很高兴。可是考完以后，每个人都考得很糟糕，大家觉得题目*一点儿也不容易。学生们又去问老师，老师说："我说得不错嘛。十分，容易；另外九十分很难啊。"

Students asked the teacher nervously before the exam, "is the exam difficult?" The teacher answered only in a sentences: "quite easy." Everyone is happy. However, everyone got a bad result after the exam, they all think the exam is not easy at all. The students asked the teacher again, the teacher said, "I didn't say something incorrectly, it is easy to get ten points, but difficult to get the other ninety points."

你知道吗？ Do You Know？（1）

送礼的习惯

送礼与受礼虽然都是我们生活中常常经历的事，但是其中的讲究你不一定知道得很清楚。在不同的国家，在不同的时候，在不同的情况下，给不同的人送什么礼，是马虎不得的。

在中国，第一次去朋友、师长家，一般带水果、点心、茶叶等。如果家里有较小的孩子，那么可以给孩子带上一盒巧克力或者孩子们喜爱的其他小食品，带上一件小玩具也会很受欢迎。

为祝贺生日，可以送一张生日贺卡，也可以买一个生日蛋糕，还可以在一起吃顿饭。当然买一件过生日的人喜爱或需要的其他小礼物，一定也会令他快乐开心。

去参加婚礼，一般送实用的生活用品，如床上用品、炊具、餐具、茶酒具等，也有送相册、镜框、鲜花的。如果对新人需要什么不太了解，又不愿新人对礼物不称心，也可以送一些钱。至于钱数的多少，就要看本人的经济状况及本人与新人的关系亲疏来决定了。另外，一般所送礼物和钱都要用红纸包好。

过春节时去亲友家拜年，可以带一些糖果、糕点。中秋节之前去探亲访友，可以买上一盒月饼。

去看望病人时，可以视病人的病情选购一些营养品、滋补品送上，或者买一些水果。现在也有不少人给病人送上一束鲜花。

如果受礼的对象是学生，则常常送些文具，如笔、笔记本等，有时还写上"祝学习进步"等勉励的话语。

为分别留念而送的纪念品，在知识界多为照片、相册、文具、书籍等，常要写上几句临别赠言，内容有祝前程远大的，有祝事业有成的，有祝友谊长存的等等。

去外地出差或旅游回来，常有人带一些外地的土特产或纪念品送给亲朋好友。

做客送礼，有人一进主人家门，就将礼物郑重送上；有人则在起身告辞时才拿出送上。送上礼物时，一般要说"一点儿小礼物，不成敬意"等客气话。受礼的人总要先推辞一番："您太客气了，带这么多礼物干什么"，"让您破费了，太谢谢了"。即使客人一进门就送上了礼物，受礼的人一般也不能当面把礼物打开。待客人离去时，才可以观看或品尝。

在中国，有些东西是不能作为礼物送给别人的，比如祝贺生日时，不能送钟。因为"送钟"与"送终"发音相同，"送终"就是给死去的人送葬，是很不吉利的；参加婚礼时，不能送伞。因为"伞"与分散的"散"同音，"散"意思是不紧密，意味着分离，新人怎能接受？看望病人时，不能送梨。因为"梨"与"离"同音，病人是很忌讳的。

以上介绍的只是一般的送礼、受礼习俗。具体什么时候送什么礼，你都清楚了吗？

The Custom of Giving Gifts

Even though giving and receiving gifts is a common experience in our lives, you might not clearly understand the specific rules. In different countries, at different time and for different people, you must be careful to give.

In China, the first time you go to a friend's or teacher's home, usually you can bring fruits, cakes, tea, etc., and if the family has a child, then you can bring the child a box of chocolates, or other snacks that the children might like, and something like a toy will be very much welcome.

To celebrate a birthday, you can give a birthday card, you could also buy a birthday cake or have dinner with them. Of course, buying a little gift that the person likes or needs could definitely make that person happy.

When going to a wedding ceremony, generally give a practical gift like bed linen, cutlery, kitchenware, and there's also glassware, photo albums, picture frames, or flowers. If you don't really know what the newlyweds need, and if you're not sure whether it's to the newlyweds liking or not, you could also give them money. And as far as the amount of money is concerned, you should take into consideration your own financial situation and your relation with the newlyweds. In addition, generally gifts or money should be wrapped in the red paper.

When visiting friends and relatives to celebrate Spring Festival, you could bring some candy or cakes; and when visiting friends and relatives before the Mid-autumn festival, you could buy a box of mooncakes.

When going to visit someone in the hospital, you could buy some nutritious things depending on the patient's condition; generally these are fruits. Now many people also buy the patients flowers.

If the person receiving a gift is a student, then stationery products such as pens, notebooks, etc., can be given, and sometimes one would also write encouraging words inside like "Wishing you progress in your studies".

The majority of parting souvenir gifts in intellectual circles are photos, photo albums, stationery, and books, etc., often with words of advice written upon them, the contents of which include wishes for a bright future, success in business, or long-lasting friendship, etc.

When returning from a long business trip or travel, people often bring back specially produced products or souvenirs to give to close friends and family.

As a guest giving gifts, as soon as you enter the host's home, then you solemnly present the gift; some people, however, wait until leaving to present their gift. When presenting the gift, generally one needs to say such niceties as "I'm embarrassed to give such a small gift" etc. People receiving gifts always need to refuse first by saying, "You're too polite, what are you doing bringing so many gifts!" and "Thank you for going to such an expense." Even though a guest may present a gift as she/he enters, the recipient generally can't open it in front of her/him, but when the guest is about to leave, one can then take a look.

In China, some things cannot be used as gifts, for example, when giving birthday presents, you shouldn't give a clock because of the similarity in pronunciation of "送钟" (sòng zhōng, to give a clock) and "送终" (sòng zhōng, to make funeral arrangements). "送终" means to join a funeral procession, it's very inauspicious; when attending a wedding, don't give an umbrella, because the pronunciation of "伞" (sǎn, umbrella) is similar in pronunciation to the "散" (sàn) of "分散", and "散" means separable, and if it has the flavor of separation, how can newlyweds accept it? When visiting patients, you shouldn't give pears because of the similarity in pronunciation of "梨" (lí) and "离" (lí), patients are very fragile.

The introduction above is only general gift-giving and gift-receiving custom; gifts must be given according to specific circumstances. Do you understand now?

Kàn bǎ nǐ gāoxìng de
看把你高兴的

（在家里）

儿 子：妈妈，妈妈，好消息！

妈 妈：看把你高兴的！什么好消息？

儿 子：今天考试成绩出来了，我语文98，数学100，外语96，是全班第一名。老师表扬我了。

妈 妈：好孩子，祝贺你！妈妈今天做几个你爱吃的菜。

儿 子：我来帮您。

妈 妈：不用了，你玩儿会儿去吧。一会儿你爸爸回来，让他也高兴高兴。

儿 子：那我玩儿会儿电脑去了。

（爸爸回来了）

爸 爸：今天怎么了？有这么多好吃的。

儿 子：有好事嘛，爸爸您猜。

爸 爸：我猜不着。

妈 妈：告诉你吧，这次考试，咱儿子得了全班第一，我看他准能当三好生。

爸 爸：好儿子，说说，考了多少？

儿 子：语文98，数学100，外语96。

爸 爸：考得不错，还得继续努力啊！

儿 子：我知道，爸爸、妈妈都给我加油吧！

爸 爸：儿子，除了学习好以外，别的方面也不能落后呀。

儿 子：当然了。我是学校足球队队长，也是合唱队队员，这学期我还被选上了
班长。

爸爸、妈妈：好，好，儿子加油！

（孩子对父母说）

我们学校有很多课外活动小组，每个小组都有一位老师辅导，同学们可以
按照自己的兴趣报名参加。今天，我报名参加了合唱队，第一次参加了合唱
队的活动。辅导老师说我的声音很好，可是唱歌的方法不对。老师教了我们发
声的方法，我试了试，觉得好多了。从今天开始，我要好好儿练习，将来当一
个歌手，实现我的梦想。

注 释 Notes

1. 看把你高兴的

Let's see what's made you so happy.

这句话的意思是"看（那件事）让你高兴的（样子）"。口语中常说的有："看把你急的""看把爸爸气的""看把他们感动的""看把那个人累的"等。

The meaning of this sentence is "look at (it's because of that matter) what's made you so happy". Frequently used expressions in colloquial speech are: "看把你急的""看把爸爸气的""看把他们感动的""看把那个人累的", etc.。

2. 让他也高兴高兴

It'll make him happy, too.

形容词"高兴"重叠之后为"高兴高兴"。双音节形容词的一种重叠方式是"ABAB"。本课"让他也高兴高兴"是"（把得到好成绩的消息告诉他）让他也跟我们一样高兴"。句中用"高兴高兴"而不用"高兴"，是使高兴的意思。

The verb "高兴" becomes "高兴高兴" after reduplication. The reduplicating form of two-syllable verbs is "ABAB". "让他也高兴高兴" in this lesson means "(tell him the news that you achieved a good score) and make him as happy as we are". The use of "高兴高兴" instead of "高兴" means to make someone happy.

3. 三好生

a "three goods" student

"三好生"是"三好学生"的简称。"三好"的内容是"思想品质好、学习好、身体好"。自 20 世纪 50 年代起，中国的中小学校，每年开展评选"三好生"的活动，以鼓励学生积极进取、努力学习、锻炼身体，争取在德、智、体几方面全面发展。

"三好生" is an abbreviation of "三好学生". The contents of the "three goods" are "good moral character", "good studies", and "good health". Since the 1950s, middle schools and primary schools in China have initiated "'three goods' students" movements in order to encourage students to do physical exercise, study hard, and to cultivate oneself from the perspectives of morals, intelligence, and health.

4. 除了学习好以外，别的方面也不能落后呀

Aside from studying hard you can't fall behind in other matters either.

介词"除了"跟"还、也"等连用，表示在所说的之外，还有别的。用"除了"的分句，有时也说"除了……以外"。如：

Proposition "除了" and "还，也" are used together, expressing in addition to that already mentioned, there is still additional information. The clause containing "除了" also sometimes is said "除了……以外". For example:

（1）除了味道好，价钱也很便宜。

（2）他除了上课以外，还辅导别人英语。

练　习　Exercises

一 用正确的语调读句子 Read the following sentences in correct intonation

1. 看把你高兴的！什么好消息？

2. 有这么多好吃的？

3. 咱儿子得了全班第一，我看他准能当三好生。

4. 好孩子，祝贺你！

5. 从今天开始，我要好好儿练习。

6. 将来当一个歌手，实现我的梦想。

二 根据课文内容用自己的话回答问题

Answer the questions in your own words according to the content of the text

1. 儿子说的好消息是什么？

2. 爸爸妈妈为什么那么高兴？

3. 那个学生的梦想是什么？

4. 为了实现梦想，那个学生现在是怎么做的？

三 替换句中画线部分的词语 Substitute the underlined words in the sentences

1. 看把你高兴的！什么好消息？

累	干什么去了？
美	什么事这么开心？
辣	不能吃就别吃了。
气	一点儿小事，不值得生气。
急	光急是没有用的。

2. 让他也<u>高兴高兴</u>。

辛苦辛苦
舒服舒服
凉快*凉快
轻松轻松
痛快*痛快

3. 我看<u>他</u>　　　　准　　　　<u>能当三好生</u>。

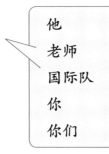

他
老师
国际队
你
你们

知道这件事
先到
能赢
记错了
猜不对

4. 从<u>现在</u>起，　　　　<u>就要做好准备</u>。

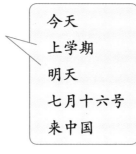

今天
上学期
明天
七月十六号
来中国

我们就是朋友了
我们就开这门课了
我们就换新老师
开始放暑假
我就想一定学好汉语

5. <u>好</u>极了，为你加油！

棒
热
辣
舒服
紧张

真为你高兴！
快休息休息。
少吃点儿吧。
想再躺一会儿。
忘了他的名字。

四　在括号里填上合适的动词，组成词组并说一句完整的话

Fill in the brackets with proper verbs to make phrases and then make a complete sentence

（　　）三好生　　（　　）课外活动小组　　　　（　　）准备
（　　）问题　　　（　　）兴趣　　　　　　　　（　　）梦想
（　　）身体　　　（　　）方法

五　谈一谈 Have a talk

1. 你小时候考试考得好时，爸爸、妈妈会有什么表示*？
2. 你小时候考得不好的话，爸爸、妈妈会怎么样？
3. 你的学校有课外活动小组吗？请介绍介绍。
4. 你对什么有兴趣？你参加过什么课外活动小组？

六　演讲 Speech

我的梦想

My Dream

七　辩论 Discussion

甲方*：考试成绩是最重要的

乙方*：学习过程*是最重要的

Side A: The result of the exam is the most important

Side B: The process of study is the most important

八　说一说，笑一笑 Talk and laugh

谁傻*

一个来旅游的人，路过一家商店，进去问老板："先生，您窗户上的广告写错了字，您为什么不改过来，难道*是没注意到吗？"

"说实话，因为有了这个写错了字的广告，人们都以为我傻，所以都来我这里买东西。我得感谢这个广告，为什么要改它的错呢？"

Who is silly

A traveler passed by a shop, went into it and asked the boss, "Sir, there is a wrongly written character in the advertisement on your window, why don't you correct it? Haven't you noticed it before?"

"Tell you honestly, people all think that I'm silly after they see the wrongly written character in this advertisement, so they all come in and buy my goods. Thanks to this advertisement, and why should I correct it?"

Duìbuqǐ, wǒ lái wǎn le
对不起，我来晚了

（在电影院门口）

男：对不起，我来晚了。等急了吧？

女：你怎么又迟到了？看看表，都几点了？

男：实在对不起！快要下班的时候，老板让我复印几份东西，我用最快的速度
复印完了。出来时，发现自行车没气了。打辆的吧，又碰上堵车。你说倒霉
不倒霉？

女：你总是有那么多理由。

男：好了，别生气了，原谅我吧。下回……

女：每次约会你都迟到，下回谁还相信你呀？你以为我有的是时间等你呀。

41

男：别动！快拿镜子来！

女：干什么？

男：照照你生气的样子，可好看了。

女：（笑）你呀……

（在女生宿舍里）

甲：怎么还不睡呀？

乙：睡不着。愿意陪我聊聊吗？

甲：当然。我猜你一定有心事了。

乙：我给我妈写了封 E-mail，告诉她我有男朋友了。可告诉她以后，我又有些担心。

甲：她一定为你高兴，你担心什么呢？

乙：她高兴我知道。可是我担心的是另一方面。

甲：哪方面？

乙：我们俩不是一个国家的人，文化背景、生活习惯都不一样，我妈妈一定不同意我的选择。

甲：你没听说过"爱是不分国界的"吗？重要的是你们俩真心相爱。虽然文化不同、习惯也不同，可是你们俩在一起，不是很幸福吗？这就够了，不要管别人怎么想。

乙：可是我妈不是别人哪！

甲：正因为是妈妈，她才更希望你快乐幸福。你应该想办法让她明白：他是你最理想的爱人，你们俩在一起真的很合适，光担心是不能解决问题的。

乙：你说得对，今年暑假我一定带他去见见我妈。我相信他会得满分。

（女生乙给母亲打电话）

妈妈，您的 E-mail 我收到了。我早就想到您会不同意。请您听听我的想法：他虽然是外国人，但是他愿意尊重咱们的民族习惯。还有就是他受过很好的教育，人好，心好，性格好，周围的朋友也都不错。您说我夸他？不是。暑假的时候，我带他回家看看您。见了面，您就会相信他确实是个值得我爱的人了。

注　释　Notes

1. 老板让我复印几份东西

The boss wanted me to copy something.

"东西"泛指各种具体的或抽象的事物。在这里"东西"指的是"文字材料"。其他如：

"东西" generally refers to specific or abstract things. What "东西" indicates here is "文字材料"(written materials). Other examples:

（1）我不戴眼镜，什么东西也看不清楚。

（2）这两天我不太舒服，不想吃东西。

（3）口语这东西，不多说不行。

2. 你总是有那么多理由。

You've always got so many excuses.

副词"总是"有时说成"总"，表示过去经常这样，现在仍然是这样。如：

The adverb "总是" is sometimes said "总". It expresses in the past it was often a certain way, and presently it is still that way. For example:

（1）有了心事以后，他总是睡不着。

（2）上下班时，这条路总是堵车。

3. 爱是不分国界的

Love is not limited by national boundaries.

这句话的意思是说：爱情不受国界的限制，不同国家、不同种族的人，相互间都有相爱的自由。

This sentence means, the love between people is not limited by their nationalities. People of different nationalities and races have the freedom to love each other.

4. 我相信他会得满分

I believe he'll be accepted.

"得满分"原指得到规定的最高分数。在这里是比喻一切令人满意、无可挑剔。

"得满分" originally refers to obtaining the full marks by regulation. Here it indicates completely satisfying someone and unable to find any fault.

5. 心好

"心"即"心眼儿""心地"，指人的内心。"心好"指善良、坦白，对人友好，乐于助人等。

"心" means "心眼儿""心地", referring to one's inner world. "心好" indicates one is kindhearted, honest, friendly and ready to help others.

练　习 Exercises

一 用正确的语调读句子 Read the following sentences in correct intonation

1. 对不起，我来晚了。
2. 你怎么又迟到了？看看表，都几点了？
3. 你说倒霉不倒霉？
4. 你总是有那么多理由。
5. 你以为我有的是时间等你呀。
6. 愿意陪我聊聊吗？
7. 你没听说过"爱是不分国界的"吗？
8. 这就够了，不要管别人怎么想。
9. 我早就想到您会不同意。
10. 您说我夸他？不是。

二 根据课文的内容回答问题

Answer the following questions in your own words according to the content of the text

1. 男青年为什么迟到了？

2. 男青年为什么要女青年拿镜子来？她真的拿镜子来了吗？

3. 女生乙为什么睡不着？

4. "爱是不分国界的"这句话是什么意思？

5. 女生乙的男朋友怎么样？

三 替换句中画线部分的词语 Substitute the underlined words in the sentences

1. <u>打辆的吧，又碰上堵车</u>。你说　　　<u>倒霉</u>　不　　<u>倒霉</u>？

办个手续要填*好几张表*	麻烦	麻烦
一个星期上二十几节课	忙	忙
房间里什么都有	方便	方便
想睡到几点就睡到几点	舒服	舒服
我忘了带钱包	糟糕	糟糕

2. <u>你</u>总是<u>有那么多理由</u>。

他	穿得很少
老师	笑着回答学生的问题
她	睡不着
孩子	喜欢甜的
她	迟到

3. <u>你</u>　　　每　<u>次约会</u>　都　<u>迟到</u>。

我	天早上	不吃早饭
班上	个同学	有手机
我们	个星期天	出去
他们	年春节	回老家过
学校	学期	有假期

4. <u>你以为我</u>　　　　有的是　　　<u>时间等你呀</u>。

他家
放了假
在这儿住了几年
解决这个问题
他每次迟到

钱
时间去旅行
朋友
办法
理由

5. 你没听说过"<u>爱是不分国界的</u>"吗？

饭后百步*走，活*到九十九
妻管严*
时间就是金钱*
站得高，看得远
家和万事兴*

6. 正因为<u>是妈妈</u>，　　　　<u>她才更希望你快乐幸福</u>。

老师选择了我
是好朋友
关心你
不明白
尊重你

她才不高兴
我才这么不客气
才问你的情况
我才来问你
我们才请你决定

7. <u>我</u>　　　　早就　<u>想到您会不同意</u>。

我
他们俩
我们
我
我们

想跟你合作了
有过多次约会了
了解这个情况了
有这个想法
原谅他了

四　说一说下面的几个句子中"东西"的意思

Talk about the meanings of"东西"in the following sentences

1. 这条街是东西方向的。
2. 你能分清楚东西南北吗？
3. 下午我想去逛逛街，买点儿东西。
4. 这是我从家乡带来的东西，你尝尝吧。
5. 这是大人的东西，孩子别随便拿。
6. 这小东西，笑的样子真可爱*。
7. 你看看我写的东西行不行？
8. 电影里那几个穿黑衣、戴墨镜*的人都不是好东西。
9. 请帮我复印几份东西。

五　模拟表演第一段对话　Perform Dialogue 1

六　读下面的一段话，用所给的词语填空

Read the following passage and fill in the brackets with the given words

| 为 | 收 | 光 | 对 | 正 | 祝 |
| 以后 | 尊重 | 心事 | 选择 | 只要 | 有的是 |

　　女生乙的妈妈对女儿说：

　　你的 E-mail 我（　　）到了，你的（　　）妈妈都知道了。不是妈妈不同意你的（　　），（　　）因为是妈妈，所以才会（　　）你多想一想。你身边的男孩子（　　），你怎么非找一个外国人不可呢？虽然说"爱是不分国界的"，可是结婚以后的生活（　　）有爱是不够的。你们的生活习惯不同，（　　）就会知道过好家庭生活不是件容易的事。当然，这只是妈妈的想法，（　　）他真的（　　）你好，你们是真心相爱，妈妈（　　）你的选择。（　　）你们快乐幸福。

七　理解下面动词的含义，填上适当的宾语

Learn the meanings of the following verbs, fill in each bracket with a proper object and then make a complete sentence

拿（　　）　　照（　　）　　夸（　　）　　尊重（　　）　　同意（　　）

得（　　）　　想（　　）　　陪（　　）　　解决（　　）　　发现（　　）

八　谈一谈　Have a talk

1. 和别人约会，你迟到过吗？能不能谈谈当时的情况？
2. 要是别人约会迟到，你生气吗？为什么？
3. 在你们国家，年轻人交朋友（男或女）要得到父母的同意吗？要是父母不同意，一般是为什么？最后一般怎么解决？

九　成段表达　Narration

夸朋友

Praise your friend

十　说一说，笑一笑　Talk and laugh

为什么不戴手表？

　　一个人抱*着一座又老又大的座钟去修理*。走到路口向左拐的时候，跟对面走来的另一个人相撞，把那个人撞倒在地上。"真抱歉！"抱座钟的人说。被撞倒的人爬起来，说："你为什么不能像别人那样戴一块手表呢？"

Why don't you wear a watch?

A man was carrying a large and old clock to have it repaired. When he was turning left at the crossing, he knocked down another person who was coming from the opposite. "Oh, I'm really very sorry", said the man carrying the clock. The other person climbed up from the ground and said, "Why couldn't you wear a watch, just like others?"

Jiànkāng hé kuàilè bǐ shénme dōu zhòngyào
健康 和快乐比什么 都 重要

（外国人甲跟中国人乙聊天儿）

甲：我发现中国的老人挺爱跳舞的。

乙：你怎么发现的？

甲：每天不论早上还是傍晚，在公园里，总能看见跳舞的老人，他们穿得红红绿绿的，挺有意思。

乙：老人也不是人人都爱跳舞。很多爱动的老人，更喜欢爬爬山、散散步什么的。

甲：不爱动的老人做什么？

乙：有的画画画儿、练练书法，有的帮儿女带带孩子。

甲：我看，爱动不爱动都不重要，重要的是心不能老，心一老比什么都可怕。

乙：对。我常常看到外国的老人来中国旅游，年纪那么大了，头发都白了，可是精神非常好，让谁看了都羡慕。

甲：这样的人当然幸福，不过能出来旅游的并不多。

乙：一般的老人怎么过呢？有人去养老院吗？

甲：有。但是有的老人不愿意去，他们觉得在哪儿也不如在家好。

（在家里）

儿 子：妈妈，您怎么哭了？

妈 妈：没什么，是刚才看电视看的。

儿 子：什么电视让您这么感动？

妈 妈：电视里说：有一位老人，她丈夫死了好多年了。她辛辛苦苦把孩子们都带大了。有一位老先生对她好，想和她组成新的家庭，可是儿女们都反对，她受不了，结果自杀了。

儿 子：他们的儿女怎么不多为父母想想，他们不希望父母幸福吗？

妈 妈：是啊，真能理解老人的年轻人不多呀。

儿 子：说到这儿，我正有件事要跟您商量呢。

妈 妈：什么事？这么认真的样子。

儿 子：人家刘伯伯对您那么好，经常关心和照顾您，对您也有那个意思，您怎么不考虑考虑？

妈 妈：这个……，我知道他的意思，可是……

儿 子：您担心什么呀？

妈　妈：我是担心你有想法。我觉得有你就够了。

儿　子：可是儿子的爱代替不了丈夫的爱呀。

妈　妈：还有，别人怎么看呢？

儿　子：老人也有再婚的自由，您别怕这怕那的。您自己感觉幸福就够了，不要管别人怎么看。我真心希望您过得幸福、快乐！

（一位快乐的老人说）

　　人们常问我，为什么不把钱存在银行里。我是怎样想的呢？我现在身体还不错，没什么大病，我要多尝些没尝过的东西，多去些好玩的地方看看。要是等老得走不动了，牙也掉光了，再用这些钱打针、吃药、住医院，那多没意思呀？除了吃和玩以外，剩下的钱我就捐出去。我没儿没女，这些钱留着，死了也带不走，还不如帮助穷孩子上学呢。把钱用在有用的地方，我心里特别高兴。人老了才知道，健康和快乐比什么都重要。

注　释　Notes

1. 不过能出来旅游的并不多。

But there aren't so many people who can go out.

副词"并"只能放在否定词"不、没"等前边，加强否定的语气。如：

The adverb "并" can only appear in front of the negatives "不、没", strengthening the tone of the negation word. For example:

（1）我知道，我的汉语说得并不好。

（2）他并没吃饭，却说吃了。

2. 人家刘伯伯对您那么好

Uncle Liu is so good to you.

代词"人家"在这里是称说话人与听话人以外的人，所说的人已在文中出现，相当于"他"或"他们"。如：

The pronoun "人家" here is the address for somebody aside from the speaker and hearer. The person referred to already appeared in the text/conversation, and is comparable to ""他" or "他们"". For example:

（1）他正准备考试，人家没空儿跟你玩儿。

（2）人家杰夫说的汉语才棒呢。

3. 对您也有那个意思

also has those feelings towards you

"那个意思"是一种委婉的说法，常用来委婉地表示男女之间的爱慕之情。本课是指刘伯伯有与那位母亲建立新家庭的想法。

"那个意思" is a kind of euphemism, frequently used in gently expressing feelings of adoration between men and women. In this lesson it indicates the thoughts of Uncle Liu about setting up a new family with the mother.

4. 您别怕这怕那的

You needn't be afraid of this or that.

这句话的意思是：什么人、什么事您都不用怕，不要有顾虑。句中的"这""那"指代所怕的人或事物。"V 这 V 那"常用于口语中。再如：

This sentence means you needn't be afraid of anybody or anything, just don't worry. "这" and "那" in the sentence refer to the people or things that the mother is afraid of. "verb+这 +verb+ 那" is often used in oral Chinese. Other examples:

（1）我一逛商店就爱买这买那的。

（2）他一边看电视，一边还吃这吃那的。

练 习 Exercises

一 用正确的语调读句子 Read the following sentences in correct intonation

1. 健康和快乐比什么都重要。

2. 你怎么发现的？

3. 一般的老人怎么过呢？

4. 在哪儿也不如在家好。

5. 什么电视让您这么感动？

6. 他们的儿女怎么不多为父母想想？

7. 您别怕这怕那的。

8. 我真心希望您过得幸福、快乐！

二 根据课文内容回答问题 Answer the questions according to the content of the text

1. 为什么外国人觉得中国老人爱跳舞？

2. 课文中谈到的老人生活一般有哪些内容？

3. 妈妈为什么哭了？她看了什么电视节目？

4. 妈妈和刘伯伯是什么关系？

5. 儿子要和妈妈谈什么事？他妈妈为什么不想考虑这件事？

6. 那位快乐的老人为什么不存钱？他的钱都怎么用？

三 读一读，体会各句中"意思"的不同含义

Read the sentences and learn the different meanings of " 意思 "

1. 这个词是什么意思？

2. 这是我的一点儿小意思。

3. 你说这话是什么意思？

4. 那个男生好像对你有点儿意思。

5. 真不好意思，给您添了这么多麻烦！

6. 送点儿小礼物，意思意思就行了。

7. 他这个人真有意思。

8. 这样做，就不够意思了。

四 替换句中画线部分的词语 Substitute the underlined words in the sentences

1. <u>健康和快乐</u>　　比　　<u>什么</u>　都　<u>重要</u>。

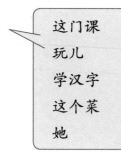

这门课	哪门	有意思
玩儿	干什么	快乐
学汉字	什么	难
这个菜	哪个菜	好吃
她	谁	漂亮

2. 她们穿得红红绿绿的，　　　挺　　　　　有意思。

他每天都高高兴兴的 我们天天忙上课、忙考试 我的房间干干净净 字写得认认真真 爸爸妈妈辛辛苦苦

快乐 紧张的 舒服 清楚的 不容易

3. 心一老　　　比　什么　都　可怕。

睡觉 面试*时，我 那里 互相理解 这个节目

什么时候 谁 什么地方 什么 哪个节目

幸福 紧张 美 重要 精彩

4. 能出来旅游的人并不多。

这里的冬天 公共汽车里 学习普通话 汉语说得好的人 我

冷 太挤 难 多 相信这样的事

5. 在哪儿　　　　也不如在家好。

干什么事 去哪儿玩儿 坐什么 住在谁家 谁做的菜

不干事轻松 在家睡觉舒服 坐飞机快 住在自己家随便 妈妈做的菜好吃

6. 什么<u>电视</u>　　　让　您　这么<u>感动</u>?

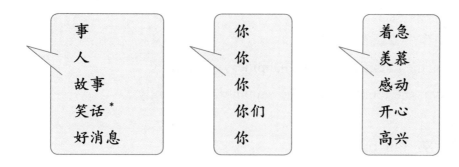

事
人
故事
笑话*
好消息

你
你
你
你们
你

着急
羡慕
感动
开心
高兴

7. 什么事?这么<u>认真</u>的样子。

着急
高兴
担心
开心
难过*

8. <u>老人也有再婚的自由</u>,　　您　别　怕　这　怕　　　那的。

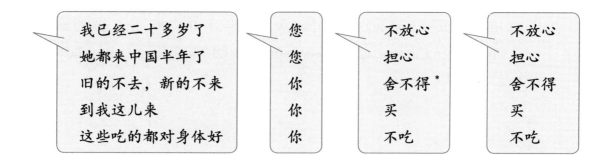

我已经二十多岁了
她都来中国半年了
旧的不去,新的不来
到我这儿来
这些吃的都对身体好

您
您
你
你
你

不放心
担心
舍不得*
买
不吃

不放心
担心
舍不得
买
不吃

五 谈一谈 Have a talk

1. 你看见过在公园里跳舞的老人吗?你觉得怎么样?

2. 在你们国家,退休老人一般的生活怎么样?他们去养老院吗?

3. 在你们国家,老人再婚的事多吗?对这样的事,一般人有什么看法?儿女对父亲或母亲再婚有什么看法?

六 成段表达 Narration

谈谈你对幸福的看法。

Talk about your opinion about happiness.

七 小辩论 Mini Debate

甲方：爱情*是家庭幸福的基础*

乙方：金钱是家庭幸福的基础

Side A: Love is the foundation of the happiness of a family

Side B: Money is the foundation of the happiness of a family

八 说一说，笑一笑 Talk and laugh

补习*广东话

甲：教授*天天到王先生家去做什么？

乙：帮助王先生和他夫人*补习广东话。

甲：他们为什么要补习广东话？

乙：因为他们收养*了一个半岁的广东小女孩，要是他们不学广东话，那么等到孩子长大说话的时候，他们就听不懂她说的话了。

Learning Cantonese

A: Why does the professor go to the Wang's everyday?

B: To help Mr. Wang and his wife learn Cantonese.

A: Then why do they learn Cantonese?

B: Because they have adopted a half-year old girl who was born in Guangdong. If they don't learn Cantonese, they won't understand what the girl says when she grows up!

Zhōumò zěnme guò?
周末 怎么 过?

（周五下班后，两个同事在回家路上）

甲：周末怎么过？

乙：回家看爸妈。

甲：你好像每个周末都回去。

乙：是啊，大家在一起热闹。做做饭，看看电视，收拾收拾房间，饭桌上一起

聊聊天儿。

甲：不想自己轻松轻松？

乙：想是想，可是一想起他们在家里等着，就不好意思自己玩儿去了。

甲：大家一起出去玩儿也可以呀。

乙：我爸我妈不爱活动，还说出去玩儿是乱花钱，他们看不惯。

甲：有时候花点儿钱出去玩儿玩儿，快乐地过个周末也是值得的。

乙：你说得有道理，可是他们觉得这样花钱不值得。

甲：老年人和年轻人的想法太不一样了，这就是他们之间的代沟吧？

乙：可能是吧。

甲：那你就在家里待着吗？

乙：在家里，我爱听我爸爸讲他过去的经历。我觉得，和他们一起过周末，常常能学到一些书本上学不到的东西，也挺有收获的。

（周日，在家中）

女 儿：妈，您又在洗衣服？我来吧。

妈 妈：马上就洗完了。你先去吃水果吧，知道你回来，我已经给你准备好了。

女 儿：您怎么不用洗衣机洗呀？

妈 妈：几件衣服，用洗衣机又费电、又费水。

女 儿：那买洗衣机有什么用？

妈 妈：我用手洗惯了，洗几件衣服还是锻炼身体呢。

女 儿：那好吧，我只好听您的，但是千万别把您自己累坏了。要不，您就得听我的了。

（周一在上班路上）

甲：你周末怎么过的？

乙：星期六和妻子、孩子一起回家看父母，星期天三口出去玩儿。

甲：安排得不错嘛。你去哪儿玩儿了？

乙：上午去了动物园，下午去附近的商场逛了逛。

（一个年轻人说）

　　周末怎么过？每个人都不一样。有的人喜欢全家团聚，大家一起做些好吃的饭菜，聊聊一周来的新闻；有的人喜欢出去玩儿，爬爬山、钓钓鱼什么的；年轻人都忙着约会；有些做父母的为了培养教育孩子，只好利用周末带孩子去各种辅导班。我呢，最喜欢周六去看展览，各种展览我都喜欢看。紧紧张张看一天，周日就痛痛快快睡懒觉，想睡到几点就睡到几点。

注　释　Notes

1. "周末怎么过"和"周末怎么过的"

　　"周末怎么过"是过周末之前提出的问题，"周末怎么过的"是过了周末之后提出的问题。两句话只差一个"的"字，意思却完全不同。

　　"周末怎么过" (How will you spend the weekend?) is a question asked before the weekend. "周末怎么过的" (How did you spend the weekend?) is a question asked after the weekend. The difference between the two sentences is only in the use of "的", but the two sentences are used at totally different time when communicating.

2. 那好吧，我只好听您的了。

　　Fine, do it your way.

　　副词"只好"表示没有别的办法了，是"不得不""只得"的意思。如：

　　The adverb "只好" expresses one has no other choice, it has the same meaning as "不得不""只得". For example:

　　（1）生病了，只好听大夫的。

　　（2）雨下得太大了，我只好等一会儿再走。

3. 要不，您就得听我的了。

　　Otherwise, you're going to have to do it my way.

　　"要不"连词，在这里的意思相当于"或者、要么"，作用是引出与上文相似或相反的情况，以供选择。后面常有副词"就"呼应。如：

　　"要不" is a conjunction, whose meaning here equals to "或者、要么". The effect is to elicit the condition which is similar or opposite to the context above for a choosing. It's often echoed by an adverb "就". For example:

　　（1）咱们到我房间里坐坐，要不就去公园散散步。

　　（2）甲：食堂买饭的人太多了，我不想等了。

　　　　　乙：要不，去饭馆吃饺子吧。

4. 聊聊一周来的新闻

　　Talk about the news of the last week.

　　"来"放在表示时段的时间词语之后，表示从过去到现在的一段时间。如：

　　"来" is preceded by a time word that expresses a period of time, indicating a period from the past until now. For example:

　　（1）几天来，一直感冒。

　　（2）快考试了，得复习复习一个月来的学习内容。

Exercises

一 用正确的语调读句子 Read the following sentences in correct intonation

1. 周末怎么过？
2. 不想自己轻松轻松？
3. 大家一起出去玩儿也可以呀。
4. 你说得有道理。
5. 老年人和年轻人的想法太不一样了。
6. 您又在洗衣服？我来吧。
7. 那买洗衣机有什么用？
8. 要不，您就得听我的了。
9. 安排得不错嘛。

二 根据课文内容回答问题 Answer the questions according to the content of the text

1. 同事乙一般怎么过周末？
2. 同事乙的父母为什么不和孩子们一起出去玩儿？
3. 妈妈为什么不用洗衣机洗衣服？
4. 甲为什么说乙的周末安排得不错？
5. 那个年轻人在介绍周末生活时都说了什么？

三 仿照例句，用加点的词语完成并扩展句子

Follow the examples to complete and extend the sentences by using the dotted words

1. 他们看不惯。→我爸我妈说，出去玩儿是乱花钱，他们看不惯。

喝
穿
听
用
吃

2. 我洗惯了。→我洗惯了，洗几件衣服还是锻炼身体呢。

骑
看
住
说
写

3. 我只好听您的。→那好吧，我只好听您的。

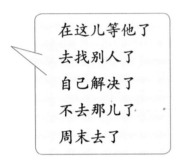

在这儿等他了
去找别人了
自己解决了
不去那儿了
周末去了

4. 要不，您就得听我的了。→千万别把自己累坏了，要不，您就得听我的了。

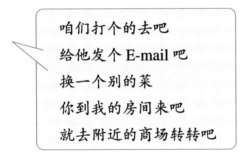

咱们打个的去吧
给他发个 E-mail 吧
换一个别的菜
你到我的房间来吧
就去附近的商场转转吧

5. 聊聊一周　　来　　的新闻。→大家一起做些好吃的饭菜，聊聊一周来的新闻。

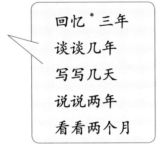

回忆 *三年
谈谈几年
写写几天
说说两年
看看两个月

的学习生活
的变化
的想法
的经验
的成绩

6. 想睡到几点　　　　　　就睡到几点。→周日就痛痛快快睡懒觉，想睡到几
点就睡到几点。

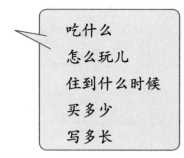

吃什么
怎么玩儿
住到什么时候
买多少
写多长

吃什么
怎么玩儿
住到什么时候
买多少
写多长

四　读例句，体会加点词语的意思并模仿对话

Read the examples, and learn the meanings of the dotted words and perform the dialogues

1. 甲：周末不想自己轻松轻松？
　　乙：想是想，可是一想起他们在家里等着，就不好意思自己玩儿去了。

2. 甲：我爸我妈不爱活动，还说出去玩儿是乱花钱。
　　乙：有时候花点儿钱出去玩儿玩儿，快乐地过个周末也是值得的。

3. 甲：有时候花点儿钱出去玩儿玩儿快乐地过个周末也是值得的。
　　乙：你说得有道理，可是他们觉得这样花钱不值得。

五　熟读下面形容词、动词的重叠形式，并用它们各造一个句子

Learn by heart the duplication forms of the following adjectives and verbs, and then make a sentence with each word

平平安安	开开心心	认识认识	关照关照
热热闹闹	快快乐乐	解决解决	活动活动
痛痛快快	认认真真	培养培养	利用利用
辛辛苦苦	安安静静	收拾收拾	提高提高

六　读下面一段话，用所给的词语填空

Read the following passage and then fill in the brackets with the words given below

总是	值得	只好	差不多	一……就……
还不如	待	忙着	不好意思	

我（　　）每个周末都回家。我爸爸、妈妈年纪大了，不爱活动。平时我们都（　　）工作，到了周末，爸爸、妈妈（　　）等着我们回家，所以，就（　　）自己出去玩儿了。有时候，我们也想请父母和我们一起出去玩儿，可是他们觉得我们（　　）出去玩儿（　　）乱花钱，不（　　），（　　）在家里（　　）着，一起聊聊天儿、做些好吃的呢。没办法，（　　）随他们的便了。

七　谈一谈 Have a talk

1. 你周末一般怎么过？
2. 在你们国家，老人一般怎么过周末？
3. 在你们国家，结婚以后有了孩子的人一般怎么过周末？
4. 有的老人认为，出去玩儿是乱花钱，不值得，你怎么看？
5. 在你们国家，家里的老人做家务*有困难怎么办？

八　讨论 Discussion

现在有的父母为了培养孩子，总是利用周末带孩子上各种辅导班。孩子们为了学习，没有玩儿的时间。你认为这些父母的做法*怎么样？他们为什么要这样做？如果你是父母，你怎样培养你的孩子？如果你是孩子，你希望周末干什么？

In order to cultivate the children, nowadays there are many parents taking their children to all kinds of tutorial classes in the weekends. The children don't have any time to play be cause of study. What do you think of the parents' behavior? What do they do this for? If you are a father or mother, how will you cultivate your child? If you are a child, what do you expect to do at weekends?

九　说一说，笑一笑 Talk and laugh

最后一次吹牛*

有个人一生*最爱吹牛。当他快要死的时候，他对家里人说："现在我说句实话吧，在我卧室*的地下*，有个盒子*，里边放着很多钱。"

那个人死后，家里人找到盒子。打开以后，发现盒子里只有一张纸条*，上面写着："这是我一生最后的一次吹牛。"

My last boast

A man likes boasting most all his life. When he was going to die, he said to his family, "Now I must tell you the truth that in the box placed under the floor of my bedroom, there is a lot of money." His family found the box after his death and only found a note in it, on which is written, "This is the last boast in my life!"

你知道吗？　Do You Know？（2）

热情与含蓄

　　绝大多数中国人都非常热情好客，乐于助人。在路上，你常常可以看到两三个人热情地交谈彼此的情况，表示相互的关心；在火车上，聊得挺热闹的一些人，其实很可能是初次相识的陌生人；你可能常从中国人那儿听到："有空儿请到家里来玩儿"。当然，只有他说出具体时间才是真正的邀请。即使偶尔有不打招呼就突然来访的人，如果不是有非常紧急的事，主人都会立即起身热情招待。中国人喜欢请朋友到自己家里做客、一起吃饭，而且通常总是准备十分丰盛的饭菜招待客人。

　　中国人对朋友的求助、邀请等，一般不直接拒绝或推辞，而是用含蓄、委婉的语言来表示。比如：当有人请你明天一起吃晚饭时，如果你不想去或不能去，你可以说："真对不起，明天晚上有一个约会，我不能去。""谢谢你的盛情！可是不凑巧，明晚我有点儿事。"再如：请客人吃饭时，主人喜欢热情地给客人布菜、让酒，希望客人多吃点儿、多喝点儿。但有的菜可能不对客人的口味，或客人酒量有限，这时客人就说："您别客气，我自己来。""不能奉陪了，已经过量了。"

　　当对某人某事不满意，需要提出自己的意见或建议时，中国人常常习惯使用商量、假设的语气，或用问句来表达。比如："这个饭馆的客人太多了，我看咱们还是去旁边的那个吧。""这么重要的事，你要是早点儿告诉我就好了。""这样写挺好的。不过我觉得那样写可能更好些，你说呢？""你汉语说得挺好的，就是声调还有点儿问题。"等。

　　如果某人、某事真的让你很生气、很不满意，你完全可以不用委婉含蓄，尽管直接表达你的意见。你遇到过这样的情况吗？

　　用委婉的词语表示亲人、朋友、所尊敬的人已经死去，是中国人自古以来的传统。这方面的委婉表达方法非常多，一般的有"去世了""不在了""老了""走了"等等。

　　中国人的热情与含蓄表现在很多方面，在"做客与待客""送礼的习惯"中也都谈到一些。你还可以用自己的眼睛去看一看，用你的耳朵去听一听，你肯定会有新发现的。

Enthusiasm and Implicitness

Most Chinese people are extremely enthusiastic, hospitable, and altruistic. In the street, you can often see two or three people enthusiastically talking about each other's situation and expressing concern for each other. On the train, actually it's very possible that some people who are talking quite animatedly are strangers who've met for the first time. You could also hear from a Chinese, "If you're free, come to my home and have fun." Of course, only when he says a specific time, it is a true request. Even though you occasionally pop up without letting them know, the host will enthusiastically treat you at once, if he hasn't got a urgent business. Chinese people really like to invite friends to their homes to be guests for dinner, and they normally prepare a sumptuous food for their guests.

Generally, Chinese don't directly refuse their friends' request or invitation, but they would rather use extremely implicit and tactful speech to express such things. For example, when someone invites you to eat dinner together tomorrow, if you don't want to go or you can't go, you can say "I'm really sorry, but I've got an appointment tomorrow night, I can't go"; "Thanks for your great kindness, but unfortunately I've got something to do tomorrow night." Also, when inviting a guest to dinner, hosts like to fill up a guest's plate and glass in the hope that the guest eats more and drinks more. But sometimes the food may not be to the guest's liking, or a guest can't handle that much alcohol. At this time a guest could say, "You are much too kind, I'll help myself"or "I am afraid that I won't be able to keep company, it is much too redundant."

If you are unsatisfied with someone or something, and you need to put forward your own opinion or suggestion, Chinese people frequently use the tone of discussion or assumption, or use questions to express. For example, "There are too many customers at this restaurant, how about if we go to the one next door?"; "It would have been better if you had told about such an important matter sooner!"; "Writing it like this is good, but I think writing it that way would be better, don't you think so?"; "You speak Chinese very well, just a little problem with your tone", etc.

If someone or something has made you angry or very unsatisfied, then you definitely needn't use tactful or implicit speech; just feel free to directly speak out. Have you ever encountered such a situation?

Using tactful words to express the death of family members, friends, and other respected people is an ancient Chinese tradition, and there are many different ways to express ineuphemism such as. "去世了", "不在了", "老了", "走了", etc.

Chinese people's enthusiasm and implicitness are indicated in many aspects, and we've talked about some of them in "Guest and Host" and "The Custom of Giving Gifts". If you can also go and see with your own eyes, you'll definitely make new discoveries.

Shénme shì zhēnzhèng de nán nǚ píngděng?
什么是 真正 的男女 平等？

（在家里）

丈 夫：你今天怎么也回来晚了？我来跟你一起做饭吧。

妻 子：回来得并不晚，到楼上张师傅家坐了会儿。他们家又吵架了。

丈 夫：他们为什么又吵了？

妻 子：张师傅一回家就躺在沙发上，边看电视边抽烟。他爱人下了班，又洗菜
又做饭。张师傅一点儿忙也不帮。

丈 夫：这就是张师傅不对了。两个人都上了一天的班，都挺累的，回到家，怎
么能光让一个人干活儿呢？

妻 子：他爱人叫张师傅帮着一起做，张师傅不做，结果把他爱人气哭了。

丈 夫：现在两个人怎么样了？

妻 子：我批评了张师傅，给他讲了男女在社会上要平等，在家庭中也要平等。
又把咱们俩的经验介绍了一下儿。

丈　夫：你没向他们夸夸我这个模范丈夫？

妻　子：正因为我夸了你，张师傅才改变了态度，向他爱人认了错，两个人一起
　　　　高高兴兴地做了一顿饭。

丈　夫：希望他们俩今后再也不因为做家务的事吵架了。你劝架劝得不错嘛！你
　　　　把咱们俩刚结婚时我的表现也告诉他们了？

妻　子：不说那些，经验从哪儿说起呀？

丈　夫：真不好意思，咱们俩的秘密全让人知道了。

（姐姐和弟弟聊天儿）

弟　弟：姐，我们要举行演讲比赛，帮我想想怎么讲。

姐　姐：演讲的题目是什么？

弟　弟："男女平等"。

姐　姐：这个问题很复杂，内容又太多，不好讲，你肯定有困难。

弟　弟：所以才请你帮我想想嘛，我不知道从哪儿讲起。

姐　姐：到处都有人谈男女平等，报上谈，电视里也谈。谈来谈去，连一个最简
　　　　单的问题也没谈清楚。

弟　弟：什么问题？

姐　姐：一般人都以为男人能做的事女人也能做，好像就是实现了男女平等了。

弟　弟：你怎么认为呢？

姐　姐：男人有男人的特点，女人有女人的特点，只在一点上讨论，那就太简单
　　　　了。

（弟弟在演讲）

"男女平等"是一个全社会都关心的话题。平等既是一个政治问题，也是一个经济问题。在现代社会，女人和男人一样走出家庭，参加工作，这就为实现男女平等打下了基础。可是目前，在社会上和家庭中，都还存在着男女不平等的现象。比如有一种说法是："女人干得好，不如嫁得好"。那么，女人怎样做才算处理好家庭和事业的关系了？怎样才能得到真正的平等呢？

……

注 释　Notes

1. 模范丈夫

model husband

人们把对家庭有很强的责任心、体贴妻子、主动多做家务的丈夫誉为"模范丈夫"。

People uphold a husband who lays great stress on responsibility of the family, who takes good care of his wife, and who takes the initiative in doing more household chores as a "model husband".

2. 谈来谈去，连一个最简单的问题也没谈清楚。

They keep talking about it but even the simplest problem hasn't been cheared up.

"V来V去"表示动作进行次数很多，后面的句子一般都表示没什么结果或结果不如人意。如：

"V 来 V 去" expresses an action has been executed many times, the sentence afterward usually expresses the lack of a desired result or no result at all. For example:

（1）找来找去，也没找到。

（2）商量来商量去，他也不同意。

3. 以为　认为

"以为"表示对人或事物作出判断，多用于与事实不符的判断。"认为"也表示对人或事物作出判断，一般只用于正面的论断。如：

"以为" indicates making judgment on a person or an affair, mostly not according to the fact.

"认为" also means making judgment on a person or an affair, generally only used in positive judgment. For example:

（1）今天他没来，我以为是他病了，后来才知道是他女朋友病了。

（2）他经常不来上课，大家都认为这是不对的。

4. 平等既是一个政治问题，也是一个经济问题。

Equality is a political issue as well as an economical one.

"既……也……"连接两个结构相同或相似的词组，后一部分表示进一步补充说明。如:

"既 …… 也 ……" links two expressions similar or same in structures, with the latter part indicating a further supplement. For example:

（1）我晚上既不喝茶，也不喝咖啡。

（2）学习汉语既要多听多说，也要多读多写。

5. 女人干得好，不如嫁得好。

Working well is not as good as marrying well.

这是一句现代流行语，是在讨论现代妇女社会地位问题时，有人提出来的一种看法。意思是一个女人工作中干得再成功，也不如嫁一个能干、有钱、有地位的丈夫好。

This is a popular modern phrase, an opinion that some people put forward when discussing the problem of modern women's social status. It means that no matter how successful a woman is at work, it's still not as good as marrying a husband who is capable, rich, and posted.

练 习 Exercises

一 用正确的语调读句子 Read the following sentences in correct intonation

1. 什么是真正的男女平等？

2. 我来跟你一起做饭吧。

3. 张师傅一点儿忙也不帮。

4. 结果把他爱人气哭了。

5. 男女在社会上要平等，在家庭中也要平等。

6. 不说那些，经验从哪儿说起呀？

7. 演讲的题目是什么？

8. 你怎么认为呢？

9. 男人有男人的特点，女人有女人的特点。

10. 只在一点上讨论，那太简单了。

二 根据课文内容回答问题 Answer the questions according to the content of the text

1. 张师傅夫妻俩为什么吵架?
2. 张师傅爱人为什么被气哭了?
3. 张师傅夫妻俩吵架时,邻居家的妻子是怎样劝他们的?结果怎么样?
4. 课文第一段中的丈夫是"模范丈夫"吗?为什么?
5. 姐姐对"男女平等"的问题有什么看法?

三 读例句,用加点的词语完成对话

Read the examples and complete the dialogues by using the dotted words

1. 例:甲:张师傅夫妻俩为什么又吵架了?

   乙:他爱人下了班,又洗菜又做饭。张师傅一点儿忙也不帮。

   (1) 你对经济方面的话题有兴趣吗?

   (2) 他的演讲对男女不平等现象批评了没有?

2. 例:甲:你的演讲题目就叫"男女平等"吧。

   乙:这么大的题目,我不知道从哪儿讲起。

   (1) 明天就要交演讲稿*了,你怎么一个字也没写?

   (2) 听说你们这次旅行非常有意思,快给我们介绍介绍。

3. 例:甲:"男女平等"是全社会都关心的话题,人们的看法有什么问题?

   乙:一般人都以为男人能做的事女人也能做,好像就实现了男女平等了。

   (1) 下午的课两点半才开始,你怎么一点半就来了?

   (2) 他们俩是同学,不是同事。

4. 例:甲:什么是真正的男女平等?你怎么认为呢?

   乙:我认为男女在社会上要平等,在家庭中也要平等。

   (1) 什么是最好的学习方法?

   (2) 你们谈恋爱*谈了好几年了,怎么还不结婚?

四 替换句中画线部分的词语　Substitute the underlined parts in the sentences

1. 他爱人叫张师傅一起做饭，张师傅不做，结果把他爱人气哭了。

孩子改不了爱吃糖的习惯	牙都坏
我让他早点儿出发，他不听	迟到
他病刚好，就忙着上班	又累病
他把约会的时间记错了	女朋友生气
老板不满意他的工作	老板不用他

2. 男女在社会上　　要　平等,在家庭中　　也要　平等。

住的	好，吃的	好
老师要求学生听说能力 *	提高，读写能力	提高
老人的习惯是	睡得早，	起得早
上班的路上	注意安全，下班的路上	注意安全
上课的时候，教室里边	安静，教室外边	安静

3. 到处都有人谈男女平等。

| 老人跳舞 |
| 人玩儿手机 |
| 朋友照顾我 |
| 孩子踢足球 |
| 好心人帮助我 |

4. 谈来谈去，连一个最简单的问题也没谈清楚。

说	说	也没说清楚
看	看	一个都不喜欢
走	走	又走回来了
想	想	我还是决定不去了
讨论	讨论	也没有好主意

5. <u>谈来谈去</u>，连<u>一个最简单的问题</u>也<u>没谈清楚</u>。

想了半天
吃完了
我刚来
逛了几个商店
在学校学习了两年

他的名字
是什么菜
东南西北
一件东西
图书馆

没想起来
不知道
不知道
没买
没去过

6. <u>平等</u>既<u>是一个政治问题</u>，　　也　是　个经济问题。

她
他
男女平等
孩子长得
抽烟

是一位好老师
不来上课
是社会问题
像爸爸
影响自己的健康

是一位好母亲
不参加考试
是历史问题
像妈妈
影响别人的健康

7. <u>女人参加工作</u>，　　就为　<u>实现男女平等</u>打下了基础。

学好语音
学好语言
学好汉语
学好英语
有个健康的身体

学好语言
学习专业
将来找工作
将来到外国留学
学习和生活

8. <u>女人干得好</u>　　不如　<u>嫁得好</u>。

这里的春天
两个人一个房间
坐公共汽车
学校食堂
我的汉语

秋天漂亮
一个人一个房间方便
坐地铁快
外边饭馆儿好吃
他说得好

五　谈一谈 Have a talk

1. 你看见过夫妻吵架吗？他们吵架的原因*是什么？

2. 你认为家务事应该谁来做？

3. 你觉得什么样的人才是"模范丈夫"？

4. 你认为现代社会实现了男女平等吗？为什么？

六　模拟表演 Perform

读第一段课文后，自己组织一组新的对话，然后表演：

Read the first paragraph, conduct a new dialogue and then perform it:

（1）　张师傅和他爱人吵架。

　　　　Mr. Zhang and his wife are quarrelling.

（2）　邻居家的妻子劝他们不要吵架。

　　　　Their neighbor's wife persuades them from quarrelling.

人物：张师傅　张师傅的爱人　邻居家的妻子

时间：下班回家以后

地点：张师傅的家

Characters: Mr. Zhang, Mr. Zhang's wife, their neighbor's wife

Time: When they come back home after work

Place: Mr. Zhang's home

七　成段表达 Narration

演讲："什么是真正的男女平等？"

What's the real equality between male and female?

八　小辩论 Mini debate

甲方：干得好不如嫁得好

乙方：嫁得好不如干得好

Side A: Working well is not as good as marrying well.

Side B: Marrying well is not as good as working well.

九　说一说，笑一笑 Talk and laugh

结婚前和结婚后的女人

女人最现实*了。结婚前，你要是不小心把头撞在玻璃*窗上，她会紧张地问："亲爱的*，你受伤了吧？"结婚后，你要是再发生这种事，她虽然一样紧张，说的却*是："我的天哪，玻璃没碎吧？"

A Woman Before and After Marriage

Women are very realistic. Before getting married, if you knocked your head against the glass window carelessly, she will ask you in a nervous tone: "Oh dear, are you ok?" However, if the same thing happens after marriage, although she might be as nervous as before, what she said will be "Oh my god, is the glass OK?"

Wǒ shì lái zhǎo gōngzuò de
我是来找工作的

（李林打电话找刘山）

李 林：喂，您好！麻烦您帮我叫一下儿刘山。

职 员：刘山？他早就不在这儿干了。

李 林：什么？他去哪儿了？

职 员：他开了一家电脑公司，自己当老板了。

李 林：真没想到。您知道怎么和他联系吗？

职 员：我给你他的手机号吧，他走以前留下的。

李 林：您等一下儿，我拿纸和笔。好了，您说吧。

职 员：……记下来了吗？

李 林： 记下来了，谢谢！

（在一家电脑公司办公室）

李 林：请问，王经理在吗？

秘 书：有什么事？我是他的秘书。

李 林：您好，我是来找工作的。我看到报纸上有贵公司的广告，所以就……

秘 书：王经理陪客人参观去了。请先把您的简历给我一份。

李 林：您看这些够吗？

秘 书：有学历证明吗？

李 林：有。这是毕业证的复印件。

秘 书：好，经理一回来，我就交给他。什么时候面试，请等我们的电话。

（公司领导们面试李林）

甲：你为什么要做这份工作？

李：我对这份工作感兴趣。

乙：现在电脑公司很多，你为什么想来我们公司？

李：你们是一家新开的公司，发展很快。我认为在这里工作有前途。

丙：你说的"有前途"是什么意思？

张：在工作中锻炼，提高工作能力和技术水平，也希望快点儿增加收入。

乙：我们这儿的工作很忙，有时候周末也不能休息。

李：我很年轻，喜欢紧张的生活。我母亲常说："不忙不幸福。"我觉得她说得有道理。

甲：今天的面试就到这儿，结果怎么样请等我们的通知。

（一位公司经理说）

我们公司每年都招一些新职员，其中有不少中年人给我留下了很好的印象。因为他们年龄比较大，都工作过一段时间，所以他们懂技术、有经验，能够很快熟悉工作，工作起来认真、负责，我对他们很满意。当然，来面试的大学毕业生也不少，有一些也成了我们的新职员。他们热情、爱学习，技术和能力都提高得很快。我对他们也很满意。

注 释 Notes

1. 贵公司

"贵"敬辞，称与对方有关的事物。如：
"贵" is a polite term of address for things or institutions related to the listener, such as:
贵姓、贵国、贵校

2. 毕业证

"证"即"证件"，证明身份、经历。如：
The "证" of "证件" is a certificate of proof of identity or experience. Such as:
学生证、身份证、出入证、结婚证

3. 不忙不幸福

not happy if not busy
这句话用"不……不……"这个二次否定格式表示肯定，意思是"忙使人感到幸福"，说明说话人对生活有一种积极进取的精神。
In this sentence the twice negation form "不……不……" is used to express affirmation. It means "being busy can make one feels happy", indicating an up-and-coming spirit and an active attitude towards life.

4. 记下来 / 工作起来

（1）"下来"用在动词后，本义表示从上到下，这里表示动作的完成或结果。如：

"下来" is used after the verb, the literal meaning indicates movement from above to below. Here it means an action's completion or result. For example:

（1）我把你的手机号记下来。

（2）新书发下来了。

（2）"起来"用在动词或形容词后，本义表示从低到高，这里表示动作或情况开始或继续。如：

"起来" is used after a verb or an adjective, its literal meaning is from low to high. Here it expresses an action or situation's execution or continuation. For example:

（1）我玩起来常常忘了时间。

（2）天气热起来了，夏天快到了。

 练　习　Exercises

一 用正确的语调读句子 Read the following sentences in correct intonation

1. 我是来找工作的。

2. 麻烦您帮我叫一下儿刘山。

3. 您知道怎么和他联系吗？

4. 请问，王经理在吗？

5. 我对这份工作感兴趣。

6. 在这里工作有前途。

7. 我很年轻，喜欢紧张的生活。

8. 我对他们很满意。

二 替换句中画线部分的词语 Substitute the underlined words in the sentences

1. 他　　　　早就　　不在这儿干了。

我	知道了
我们	认识了
他们	研究过这个问题了
秘书	把你的简历交给经理了
我	熟悉这儿的饭馆儿了

2. 记下来了吗？

价钱谈
HSK 考
课文背 *
他答应
照片拷

了吗
没有
了吗
了吗
没有

3. 人　　　不　忙　　不　　　　幸福。

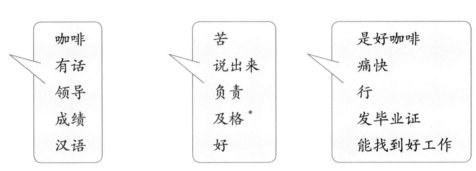

咖啡
有话
领导
成绩
汉语

苦
说出来
负责
及格 *
好

是好咖啡
痛快
行
发毕业证
能找到好工作

4. 工作起来认真、负责。

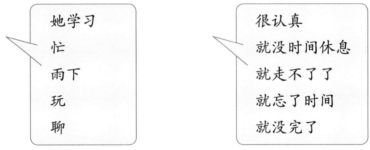

她学习
忙
雨下
玩
聊

很认真
就没时间休息
就走不了了
就忘了时间
就没完了

5. 我　　　　对　他们　　　　　很　满意。

她
我
老师
他
他们

面试
他
学生
朋友
工作

重视
了解
严格
关心
负责

三　根据课文内容回答问题 Answer the questions according to the content of the text

1. 李林为什么没找到刘山？
2. 李林找工作顺利吗？
3. 李林的面试情况怎么样？
4. 公司经理为什么对新职员很满意？

四　读例句，体会加点词语的意思并模仿对话

Read the examples, learn the meanings of the dotted words and perform the dialogues

1. 甲：他早不在这儿干了。
   乙：什么？他去哪儿了？

2. 甲：他开了一家电脑公司，自己当老板了。
   乙：真没想到。您知道怎么跟他联系吗？

3. 甲：我给你他的手机号吧。
   乙：您等一下儿，我拿纸和笔。好了，您说吧。

五　根据下边的情景设计对话 Design dialogues according to the following situations

1. 李林打刘山的手机，两个人通了电话。

   Li Lin called Liu Shan's mobile phone and they talked on the phone.

   参考词语：Words for reference:

   听说　没想到　开　公司　感觉　认为　当　老板

2. 李林和王经理秘书谈话。

   Li Lin talks with the secretary to Mr. Wang, the manager.

   参考词语：Words for reference:

   简历　准备　广告　机会　找　工作　等　交给

六　小实践 Mini practice

准备：1. 写出自己的简历。

　　　2. 问参加面试的人几个问题。

Preparation: 1. Design a resume for yourself.

2. Prepare some questions for the interviewee.

方法：分小组，每个人既参加面试，又面试别人。

Method: Divide the students into groups, with each person playing the role of interviewer as well as interviewee.

要求：1. 参加面试时，先介绍自己，再回答别人的问题。

2. 听别人的介绍，给他提一两个问题，说说对他面试的印象。

Requirement: 1. First introduce yourself and then answer the questions raised by others in the interview.

2. Listen to other person's introduction, ask him/her questions and talk about the impression that she/he gives you.

七　谈看法 Talk about your opinions

1. 开公司　　　2. 找工作　　　3. 面试

参考词语和句式　Words and sentence patterns for reference

认为	而且	因为	有前途
只要……就……	对……感兴趣	不如	利用
有意思	所以	有道理	在……中

八　说一说，笑一笑 Talk and laugh

比一比

父亲教育自己的孩子说："你应该好好学习。你知道吗？林肯*在你这个年龄的时候，是班上最好的学生。"孩子说："是啊。可我也知道，林肯在您这个年龄的时候，已经是美国总统*了。"

Have a Comparison

Father educated his child: "You should work hard. Do you know that when Lineon was of the same age as you, he was the best student in his class?" The child answered, "Yes, but I also know that when he was of the same age as you, he was already a president!"

妻管严

职员拿出最大的勇气*说："老板，我妻子说，我应该向您提出增加工资的请求*。"

"好的。我去问问我老婆*，可以不可以给您增加工资。"老板回答。

Wife's Advice

The employee was on his mettle and said to the boss: "Sir, following my wife's advice, I hope you could give a raise to my pay."

"Ok, I'll decide after I hear my wife's advice."

Qǐng nǐ cān jiā wǒmen de hūnlǐ
请 你 参 加 我 们 的 婚 礼

（两个同事在办公室）

甲： 谁的喜糖？

乙： 李秘书的。

甲： 他结婚了？什么时候办的喜事？

乙： 没办。请亲戚朋友喝了顿喜酒，然后就带着新娘旅行去了。

甲： 怪不得这几天他没来上班呢，原来是当新郎去了。他们去几天？

乙： 最少也得一个星期吧。

甲： 旅行结婚，这个办法不错。

乙： 将来你也来个旅行结婚，好不好？

甲： 我来个更浪漫的。

乙： 什么更浪漫的？

甲： 这是秘密，现在不能告诉你。

（一对恋人去王平家）

男： 王平，你好！

王平： 是你们哪，快请进！什么时候吃你们的喜糖呀？

女： 六月十六日，星期六。请你参加我们的婚礼。

王平： 这可是大喜事。日子选得真好！六六大顺哪！我一定去。喜酒得多多准

备呀。

（在婚礼宴会上）

主婚人：请大家举杯，为新郎新娘的幸福，干杯！

客人们：干杯！

主婚人：现在喜酒也喝了，父母也拜了，该干什么了？

一客人：新郎新娘介绍恋爱经过。

新　娘：别拿我们开心了。

主婚人：今天是什么日子？他们不说，行吗？

客人们：不行。

新　郎：那我先说吧。

主婚人：好，如果他说得不完全，新娘再给补充补充。

新　郎：我们俩是同班同学，原来互相不太熟悉。一天，下课的时候，突然下

　　　　起雨来……

一客人： 真浪漫。

一客人： 别说话，好好儿听。

……

主婚人： 大家说，他们的故事怎么样？

一客人： 好极了！

一客人： 太精彩了！

主婚人： 来，我们再一次举杯，祝新郎新娘和和美美！

客人们： 白头到老！

（主婚人说）

我为上百对新人主持过婚礼，今天这对年轻人的父母都是我的同事，所以我对他们俩比较熟悉。小伙子长得帅，有理想，很能干。姑娘聪明美丽，知识丰富，爱好广泛。他们真心相爱，是天生的一对。说实话，我真羡慕他们。为他们主持婚礼，我非常高兴。祝他们生活幸福！

（电视主持人说）

最近，我们从上海、北京、广州了解到，占百分之五十一的人认为"不举行婚礼就不算是结婚了"。其中占百分之六十三的人认为"在什么地方举行婚礼很重要"，占百分之三十九的人选择在饭店举行婚礼。占百分之五十的人表示"为了永远记住这幸福的一天，会选择一个有意义的好日子结婚"。这些都说明，婚姻在现代人的心中越来越受到重视。

1. 喜事　喜糖　喜酒

　　"喜事"一般指让人高兴、值得庆祝的事，也特指结婚。本课是后一个意思。"喜糖""喜酒"特指结婚时招待亲友的糖和酒。

　　"喜事" usually indicates affairs that make people happy or are worth celebrating, specifically referring to wedding. It is the latter meaning in this lesson. "喜糖" and "喜酒" specifically refers to the candy and wine served to friends and relatives at a wedding ceremony.

2. 怪不得这几天他没来上班呢，原来是当新郎去了

　　No wonder he hasn't been at work these days, he must be enjoying his honeymoon!

　　"怪不得" 表示明白了事情的原因之后恍然大悟，有时跟"原来"前后呼应。如：

　　"怪不得" expresses that one comes to a sudden realization after understanding the causes of affairs. Sometimes used in conjunction with "原来". For example:

　　（1）怪不得今天他这么高兴呢，原来他妈妈来看他了。

　　（2）她是在中国长大的，怪不得她的汉语说得这么棒呢。

　　（3）怪不得她的汉语说得这么棒呢，原来她是在中国长大的。

　　（4）甲：要上课了，她怎么回去了？

　　　　　乙：她没带书。

　　　　　甲：怪不得。

3. 六六大顺

　　"六六顺"是中国民间流传的吉语。自古以来，中国人就有崇尚偶数的习俗，把偶数看作是吉数，是美好、幸运的象征，对六和双六更加崇尚。农历初六、十六、二十六历来被认为是举行婚礼的吉日。"大"表示程度深。

　　"六六顺" is an auspicious proverb among Chinese people. Since ancient times Chinese have the custom of advocating even numbers, and have seen even numbers as propitious numbers which are symbols of beauty and good fortune. They advocate six and double-six, so the sixth, the sixteenth, and the twenty-sixth of each month in lunar calendar have always been considered as good days for weddings. "大" expresses a deep degree.

4. 父母也拜了

　　"拜父母"是中国传统婚礼仪式中的一项内容，新郎、新娘要双双拜见双方的父母，以感谢他们的养育之恩。

　　"拜父母" is a content of traditional Chinese wedding ceremony. The groom and bride must pay respects to both the bride's parents and the groom's parents, and to thank the parents of both sides for the kindness of bringing them up.

5. 别拿我们开心了

Don't make fun of us any more.

"拿……开心"表示用某人或某事物作为开玩笑、戏弄的对象。如:

"拿……开心" means making fun of somebody or something. For example:

（1）他们常常拿我开心。

（2）你们别拿我说错的话开心了。

6. 和和美美　白头到老

都是新婚颂词。表达亲友对新婚夫妇的良好祝愿。"白头到老"意思是希望夫妻共同生活一直到老，也说"白头偕（音 xié，意思是"一同"）老"。"和和美美"是"和美"的重叠，意思是家庭生活和睦美满。

These are both wedding complimentary messages, expressing the good wishes of friends and relatives to the newlyweds. The meaning of "白头到老" is a hope that the couple lives together till their old age, and is also said as "白头偕老"（偕 is read as xié, meaning 'together'）. "和和美美" is a reduplication of "和美", and means that the life of the family is harmonious and happy.

7. 天生的一对

a born match

指两个人是难得的一对好夫妻，好像是上天有意匹配的一样。全句是"天生一对，地造一双"。

Here it indicates that two people make a rarely perfect couple, seemingly intentionally arranged by god. The complete phrase is "天生一对，地造一双".

 练　习 Exercises

一　用正确的语调读句子 Read the following sentences in correct intonation

    1. 请你参加我们的婚礼。

    2. 什么时候办的喜事？

    3. 怪不得这几天他没来上班呢。

    4. 旅行结婚，这个办法不错。

    5. 现在不能告诉你。

6. 是你们哪，快请进！

7. 请大家举杯，为新郎新娘的幸福，干杯！

8. 别拿我们开心了。

9. 大家说，他们的故事怎么样？

10. 祝他们生活幸福！

二 替换句中画线部分的词语

Substitute the underlined parts in the sentences

1. <u>请亲戚朋友喝了顿喜酒</u>，**然后就**<u>带着新娘旅行去了</u>。

他喝了好多酒
她说有事
通过了面试
我工作了一年
我看了一会儿电视

醉了
走了
可以上班了
来中国了
睡觉了

2. 怪不得<u>这几天他没来上班</u>呢，原来<u>是当新郎去了</u>。

没人相信
他这么重视
他画得那么好
他们那么熟悉
她汉语这么好

他总开玩笑
这是毕业考试
他从小就学习画画儿
是同班同学
是华裔

3. <u>旅行结婚</u>， 最少 <u>也得一个星期吧</u>。

坐火车去的话
韩国同学
每个班
写八百字
一个星期

要一天一夜
占百分之五十
有两位老师
要用半个小时
有三次听写

4. 将来你也来个旅行结婚，好不好？

> 我们一起开个公司
> 在农村*买一套*房子
> 让孩子去留学
> 你当一个歌手
> 退休*了就回老家住

5. 祝新郎新娘和和美美！

> 你们白头到老
> 大家学习进步
> 爸爸妈妈身体健康
> 老师们节日快乐
> 你工作顺利

6. 说实话，我真羡慕他们。

> 没谈过恋爱
> 当不了领导
> 没有经验
> 不好意思
> 觉得太突然了

7. 不举行婚礼就不算是结婚了。

> 交简历
> 干完活儿
> 来中国
> 坐地铁
> 学汉字

> 能参加面试
> 可以下班
> 了解中国
> 知道人多挤
> 能学好汉语

三 读例句，体会加点词语的意思并模仿对话

Read the examples, learn the meanings of the dotted words and perform the dialogues

1. 甲：　现在喜酒也喝了，父母也拜了，该干什么了？

　　乙：　新郎新娘介绍恋爱经过。

2. 甲：　新郎新娘介绍恋爱经过。

　　乙：　别拿我们开心了。

四 根据课文内容，介绍一下儿中国人结婚时的一些风俗习惯

Describe some Chinese wedding custom according to the content of the text

参考词语：

新郎	新娘	喜糖	喜事	选（择）	日子	和和美美
恋爱	经过	喜酒	热闹	办	拜	祝	白头到老

五 说一说 Have a talk

1. 你们国家传统的婚礼形式是怎样的？

2. 你们国家的人一般喜欢选择什么样的日子办婚礼？

3. 在你们国家，婚礼上人们说什么祝福*的话？

六 成段表达 Narration

1. 我喜欢这样的婚礼

I like such a wedding ceremony.

2. 一个浪漫的爱情故事

A romantic love story.

七 辩论 Debate

甲方：大办婚礼很值得

乙方：大办婚礼不值得

Side A: A ceremonious wedding ceremony is worthwhile.

Side B: A ceremonious wedding ceremony is not worthwhile.

八 说一说，笑一笑 Talk and laugh

结婚纪念

一个公司老板准备跟妻子庆祝*结婚纪念日*。

"亲爱的，为了纪念咱俩结婚十年，我一定要送一件你特别理想的礼物，你

想要什么？"

"亲爱的，我只想要一件早就想要的礼物，你一定得答应我。"

"我一定答应你。说吧，想要什么？"

"我想要离婚*！"

"我的天，我可没打算花那么多钱！"

Marriage Anniversary

A boss of a company wanted to celebrate the marriage anniversary with his wife.

"Darling, I want to give you an ideal gift to celebrate our tenth year's anniversary since we got married. What do you like?"

"Sweet, then you must permit to give me a gift that I have been longing for!"

"Ok, I'm sure you'll get it. Tell me what do you want?"

"I want to divorce with you!"

"Oh my god, I didn't intend to spend that much!"

Ài shēnghuó de rén yǒngyuǎn niánqīng
爱 生 活 的 人 永 远 年 轻

（在茶馆里，外国学生跟中国人聊天儿）

外： 中国人晚上一般干什么？

中： 人跟人不一样。拿我来说吧，主要是看电视。晚上常常有好看的电视剧，一天两集。一个电视剧一般有二三十集，有的四五十集。

外： 那么长！

中： 如果好看就不觉得长。

外： 除了看电视，还干什么？

中： 已经退休的，有的打牌，有的打麻将。没退休的，拿我姐姐来说，她是教师，一般是备备课，陪孩子玩儿一会儿，再做点儿家务什么的，就差不多该睡觉了。

外： 其他年轻人呢？

中： 有的去逛逛街、跳跳舞、唱唱卡拉OK什么的，有的上网聊聊天儿。你呢？

外： 吃完晚饭先出去散散步，然后回房间复习复习白天学的新课。有的时候给家里打打电话，或者上上网、给朋友发发E-mail什么的。

（两个歌迷在聊天儿）

甲： 快来听，我下载的这首歌太好听了。

乙： 我听听，我怎么不觉得好听？老了。

甲： 你别这么说，你才比我大两岁。难道你不喜欢流行歌曲吗？

乙： 不太喜欢，主要是不常听。我还是喜欢老歌。以前的老歌，可好听了。

甲： 我发现咱们俩虽然都是歌迷，可是迷的对象大不一样。电影你爱看老的，歌曲也爱听老的。我怎么对老歌就没兴趣呢？

乙： 这没什么奇怪的，各人有各人的爱好嘛。不过，咱们有一点是相同的：咱们都爱好音乐，对吧？

（一个中年人说）

下班回家，我不是在厨房，就是在书房。我有两大爱好，一动一静，一个是做饭，一个是看书。做饭可以活动身体，看书可以丰富知识。怎么样？挺科学吧？你说我应该出去晒晒太阳？不用出去。坐在我家的阳台上，一边晒太阳，一边看书，那才舒服呢！

（一位退休老人说）

我的生活很精彩，天天过得很开心。年轻的时候，我爱好运动，经常打篮球、排球、乒乓球。我也喜欢旅行，游览了许多名胜古迹。我还做过许多种工作，当过教师、导游和律师。虽然现在已经退休了，可是我还有干不完的事。我常常去老年人活动中心，跟周围的退休老人一起健身和娱乐，好像人也变得年轻了。实践证明：爱生活的人永远年轻。

注 释 Notes

1. 拿我来说吧，主要是看电视。

Take me as an example, I mainly watch TV.

"拿……来说"表示从某个方面提出话题或以某人某事物作例子。如：

"拿……来说" used to introduce a topic from some perspective or taking somebody or something as an example. For example:

（1）西安是个旅游城市，拿名胜古迹来说，你一个星期也看不完。

（2）有的年轻人特别喜欢名牌，拿小王来说，他穿的、用的都是名牌。

2. 或者 / 还是

连词"或者""还是"都可以表示选择关系。在疑问句中，用"还是"不用"或者"。如：

"或者" and "还是" both can express a relation of choice. "还是" is used in the question instead of "或者". For example:

（1）去食堂还是去饭馆儿？你快点儿决定。

（2）你说嘛，同意还是不同意？

在陈述句中，"或者""还是"都可以用。如：

In a statement, either "或者" or "还是" can be used. For example:

不论下雨或者 / 还是刮风，他都骑自行车上班。

但是有几点要注意：

Some points that should be paid attention to:

（1）宾语表示不确定的看法时，用"还是"不用"或者"。如：

If the object expresses an indefinite opinion, "还是" is used instead of "或者", for instance:

我不知道说"儿"好还是不说"儿"好。

（2）句中供选择的各项是二选一的，是甲就不能是乙，是乙就不能是甲时，用"还是"，不用"或者"。如：

If the items for choosing are alternative, i.e., when one chooses A, he can't choose B, and vice versa, then "还是" is used instead of "或者". For example:

他是努力了，还是没努力，考试以后就清楚了。

（3）句中供选择的各项可任意选择时，用"或者"，不用"还是"。如：

When the items for choosing are optional, "或者" is optional instead of "还是". For example:

你今天来或者明天来都行。

3. 难道你不喜欢流行歌曲吗？

Don't you like popular songs?

"难道……吗"是一种反问句式，副词"难道"的作用是加强反问的语气，句末除了可以用"吗"呼应以外，也可以用"不成"来呼应。如：

"难道……吗" is a rhetorical sentence pattern, and the use of the adverb "难道" is to emphasize the rhetorical tone. At the end of the sentence, "吗" is used in conjunction with it, one can also use "不成". For example:

（1）难道有困难就不学了吗？

（2）那么远的路，难道走着去不成？

4. 下班回家，我不是在厨房，就是在书房。

I'm either in the kitchen or in the study after work.

"不是X1，就是X2"这个结构表示X1与X2两项必取其一，除了X1和X2以外，没有第三项。如：

The sentence pattern "不是X1，就是X2" expresses that of the items X1 and X2, only one can be selected. Except X1 and X2, there is no the third item. For example:

（1）我们每天不是上课就是考试，忙得很。

（2）食堂的饭不是馒头就是米饭，我想吃点儿别的。

练 习 Exercises

一 用正确的语调读句子 Read the following sentences in correct intonation

1. 人跟人不一样。

2. 拿我来说吧，主要是看电视。

3. 难道你不喜欢流行歌曲吗？

4. 我发现咱们俩虽然都是歌迷，可是迷的对象大不一样。

5. 这没什么奇怪的，各人有各人的爱好嘛。

6. 下班回家，我不是在厨房，就是在书房。

7. 我有两大爱好，一动一静，一个是做饭，一个是看书。

8. 实践证明：爱生活的人永远年轻。

二 替换句中画线部分的词语

Substitute the underlined parts in the sentences

1. 除了看电视　　　　还　　干什么？

爱逛街	爱做饭。
打篮球	打排球。
当过律师	当过导游。
上网	喜欢什么？
夸你帅	夸你唱歌好听。

2. 已经退休的，有的打牌，　　　　有的　打麻将。

留学生	住校内	住校外
这些学生	学文学	学历史 *
歌迷们	喜欢老歌	喜欢流行歌曲
服务员	服务热情	服务不热情
旅行的人	爱坐飞机	爱坐火车

3. 咱们俩虽然都是歌迷，可是迷的对象大不一样。

夜里	下雪了	早上并不冷
他	才十五岁	已经是大学生了
父母	已经退休了	并没有休息
老师	年轻	课上得很不错
我	喜欢她	从来没有告诉过她

4. 我　　　怎么对　　老歌　就　没兴趣呢？

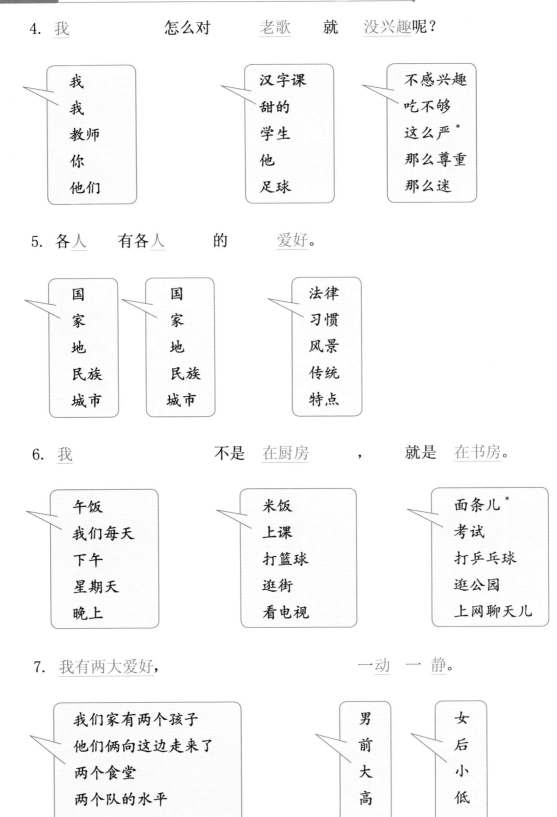

我
我
教师
你
他们

汉字课
甜的
学生
他
足球

不感兴趣
吃不够
这么严*
那么尊重
那么迷

5. 各人　有各人　的　爱好。

国
家
地
民族
城市

国
家
地
民族
城市

法律
习惯
风景
传统
特点

6. 我　　　　不是　在厨房　，　就是　在书房。

午饭
我们每天
下午
星期天
晚上

米饭
上课
打篮球
逛街
看电视

面条儿*
考试
打乒乓球
逛公园
上网聊天儿

7. 我有两大爱好，　　　　一动　一静。

我们家有两个孩子
他们俩向这边走来了
两个食堂
两个队的水平
商店门口有两个灯

男
前
大
高
左

女
后
小
低
右

8. 我还有干　　　　　不完的事。

她有洗
彼得总是有问
我们总有做
她们俩总有说
路上有看

衣服
问题
作业
话
风景

三　读例句，体会加点词语的意思并模仿对话

Read the examples, learn the meanings of the dotted words and perform the dialogues

1. 甲：中国人晚上一般干什么？
   乙：拿我来说吧，主要是看电视。

2. 甲：一个电视剧有三四十集，太长了！
   乙：如果好看就不觉得长。

3. 甲：留学生晚上都干什么？
   乙：晚饭以后散散步，然后复习复习，或者上上网、找朋友聊聊天儿。

4. 甲：年轻的时候，我也喜欢运动。
   乙：你是喜欢打球，还是喜欢游泳？

5. 甲：今年的流行歌曲我都没听过。
   乙：难道你不喜欢流行歌曲吗？

四　根据课文回答问题

Answer the questions according to the content of the text

1. 中国人晚上一般干什么？
2. 那个留学生晚上干什么？
3. 甲乙两个歌迷的爱好有什么相同？有什么不同？
4. 那个中年人的爱好是什么？
5. 那个老年人都有什么爱好？

五 体会左右两组词语不同的用法，并分别用它们说一句话或用几个说一段话

Learn the different uses of the words in two columns, make a sentence by using each word or make a paragraph with several of them

逛街——逛逛街

跳舞——跳跳舞

备课——备备课

散步——散散步

上网——上上网

聊天儿——聊聊天儿

看电视——看看电视

晒太阳——晒晒太阳

锻炼身体——锻炼锻炼身体

预习课文——预习预习课文

六 说一说 Have a talk

1. 你们国家的人晚上喜欢干什么？

2. 你最不喜欢什么运动？为什么？

3. 你有什么爱好？说说它的好处。

七 谈看法 Talk about your opinions

1. 逛街　2. 唱卡拉OK　3. 做饭　4. 晒太阳　5. 听流行歌曲

八　说一说，笑一笑 Talk and laugh

好治的病

有个人最近夜里老睡不着觉，上班没精神。他问医生："大夫，我白天很想睡觉，困*得很，可一到夜里就睡不着。您看，用什么方法能治？"大夫说："治你的病很简单，也很容易。"那个人："您快说，有什么好办法？"大夫："从今天起，你就老上夜班吧。"

Illness easy to cure

A man can't sleep well at night and has been not vigorous at work these days. He went to the doctor's and asked him: "Doctor, I'm very sleepy in the daytime, but I just can't sleep when night comes. What do you think can help me?" The doctor said, "Well, it's quite easy!" The man asked eagerly, "Then tell me please!" The doctor said, "You can just take the night shift from now on!"

你知道吗？ Do You Know? (3)

谦虚与礼让

中国人一向以谦虚为美德。当别人夸赞或推崇自己时，即使自己是当之无愧的，也一定要谦虚一番。否则，别人就会觉得你很骄傲。而骄傲在中国往往被视为"看不起别人"的同义语，是品德欠佳的表现。比如：

（1）甲："你的汉语说得挺好。"

乙："哪里哪里，还差得远呢。"

（2）甲："你的衣服真漂亮。"

乙："是吗？这是好几年前的旧衣服了。"

（3）甲："几个月不见，你越来越年轻了。"

乙："是吗？谢谢！"

除了别人夸赞时要有谦虚的表示以外，自我介绍时，也要持谦虚的态度，使用谦辞。比如：

客人来到自己的家里或宿舍，即使房间又整齐又干净，主人也常常说："家里很乱，不好意思。"而客人不管房间乱不乱，干净不干净，都会说"挺好的，挺舒服的"等客气话，表示礼貌。

请客人吃饭时，一般总是摆满一大桌。但主人仍要说："没什么菜，只是家常便饭，随便吃吧。"

送礼物给别人时，常说"这是一点儿小礼物，不好意思，请收下吧""一点儿小意思，不成敬意"等等。

在做报告或演讲时，开头常说"我的水平有限，借此机会耽误大家一点儿时间，把我的一些不成熟的意见谈一谈"。结束时，常说"我就说到这儿，说得不好，请原谅""请多提宝贵意见""不知说得对不对""说得可能不对"等等。

现在有一些年轻人受西方影响，在听到别人的夸赞或推崇时，也常常会用"谢谢"来回答，特别是对不太熟悉的朋友或在比较正式的场合。年轻人在找工作或演讲时，也喜欢实事求是地介绍自己的特长和优点。跟比较熟悉的朋友在一起时，他们甚至还喜欢吹吹牛。

Modesty and Yielding

Chinese people have always considered modesty as a virtue, and when others praise or esteem someone, even though one deserves the compliment, one should still be modest, otherwise others could feel that you are arrogant. And being arrogant in Chinese is always seen as a synonym for "looking down on others", which is a manifestation of moral degradation. For example:

(1) A: You speak Chinese really well.

B: Not at all, terrible compared to you!

(2) A: Your clothes are very pretty, are they new?

B: Really? These are some old things that I bought many years ago, they're nowhere near as pretty as yours.

(3) A: I haven't seen you in a few months, you're looking younger and prettier!

B: Really? Don't kid around, I'm old, and what's pretty about me?

Aside from being modest when others praise you, when making self-introduction, one also needs to maintain a modest attitude and make use of humble words. For example:

When a guest comes to one's home or dorm, even though the room is neat and clean, the host often says,"The place is in a mess, I'm so ashamed." And the guest, no matter the room is in a mess or clean, will always say polite things like "It's fine, very cozy" to express politeness.

When inviting a guest to a meal, generally the host always prepares many dishes. However, the host will still say, "It's not much, just some daily diet, please help yourself!"

When giving gifts to others, one often says things like, "This is just a small gift, I'm so ashamed, but please take it" or "It's just a little thing, not worth much", etc.

When making a report or giving a speech, one often says at the beginning,"My lewd is limited, I'm sorry to take your time, I'd like to discuss my immature opinions." And when concluding in the end, one often says, "I'll stop here, I haven't spoken well, please forgive me" "Please offer me suggestions""I don't know if what I've said is right" "What I've said is probably wrong", etc.

Now some young people have been influenced by the western culture, and when they hear others'compliment, they will use "thanks" as a reply, especially to somewhat unfamiliar friends or on relatively formal occasions. When job-hunting or making a speech for young people, they would like to introduce their special ties and strengths in a practical and realistic manner. When they are with relatively close friends, they even like to boast.

Wǒ shì ge yǒu kǒufú de rén
我 是 个 有 口 福 的 人

（在家里）

妻　子：咱们刚搬了新房子，请朋友们来聚聚，吃顿饭吧？

丈　夫：好啊，我建议来个自助餐。

妻　子：准备一些凉菜，再做几个热菜，谁爱吃什么就取什么。要准备酒吗？

丈　夫：当然得准备了。除了啤酒，再来点儿葡萄酒什么的。

妻　子：要不要白酒？

丈　夫：不要了吧？白酒太厉害，喝了容易醉。

（在饭桌上）

主　人：你怎么不吃啊？

客人甲：我早上起得晚，还不太饿。

主　人：你是不是在减肥？

客人甲：你别笑话我，这几个月我又长了好几斤，越来越胖了。

客人乙：你哪儿胖啊？身材多好啊！

客人甲：我真羡慕你，吃什么都长不胖。有口福啊！

客人丙：我觉得健康是最重要的。胖瘦都是给别人看的，身体好，自己觉得舒服比什么都强。

主　人：放心地吃吧，饿瘦了，脸色也不好了。要是真想瘦一点儿，最好的办法是运动。

客人甲：我也知道，可是天天坚持不容易。一停下来，会更胖。

（美国人在中国人家里做客）

男主人：中国和美国的饮食习惯很不一样吧？

美国人：是，很不一样。我喜欢吃中餐，可是有的时候很不习惯。

女主人：比如说……

美国人：喝酒的时候，主人太热情，总是让我喝。我常常不好意思不喝，有时候就喝多了。

男主人：这时候，只要你告诉他们你不能喝酒，他们不一定非让你喝不可。

女主人：如果我是你，我就说："谢谢！我不会喝酒。"或者说："我只能少来一点儿。"

美国人：好吧，以后我试试。

男主人：我去过美国。我不习惯用刀叉。左手拿叉，右手拿刀，切肉切菜，实在麻烦。吃鸡、吃鱼、吃面条儿，就更困难了。

美国人： 这就跟我们不习惯用筷子一样，不练不行。

女主人： 你们吃早饭的习惯也和我们不太一样。你们喜欢吃面包，喝从冰箱里刚拿出来的凉牛奶，同时，还要喝一些果汁。我的肚子就受不了。我习惯喝热豆浆、吃油条，再来一个煮鸡蛋。

（一个外国人说）

我是个有口福的人，吃什么都香。辣的、甜的、酸的、咸的，我都爱吃。尝尝不同风味的菜，感觉真好。我不想去麦当劳或者肯德基，因为现在我住在中国，就应该多吃中餐，这对我了解中国很有好处。只有想家的时候，我才去吃一顿西餐。

注释 Notes

1. 我是个有口福的人

I'm a person with a good appetite.

"口福"诙谐地表示胃口好，有机会、有福气吃到美味佳肴。如：可以说"有口福""很有口福""口福不浅"等。相反的意思可以说"没有口福"。

"口福" is a humorous way to express that one has a good appetite and that one is lucky to have opportunities to eat delicious food. For example, one can say "有口福""很有口福""口福不浅", etc. For the opposite meaning one can say "没有口福".

2. 他们不一定非让你喝不可

They won't necessarily force you to drink.

"非"在这里是"一定""必须"的意思，"不可"是"不成""不行"。"非"与"不可"前后呼应，用双重否定强调中间所说的那个动作必须得做，不做不行。如：

Here "非" means "一定" or "必须" ("definitely" or "necessarily"), and "不可" means "不成" or "不行" ("won't do" or "not OK"). "非" and "不可" is used together, using the double negation emphasizes that the action stated in-between must be done, without any hesitation. For example:

（1）我非学好汉语不可。

（2）你非去不可吗？

3. 不练不行

"不 V 不行"这个格式表示用双重否定强调 V 这个动作必须得做。如：

The pattern "不 +verb+ 不行" uses double negation to emphasize that the action must be done. For example:

（1）不上课不行，不上课怎么学好汉语呢？

（2）大夫说："你的病不做手术不行。"

4. 只有想家的时候，我才去吃一顿西餐。

Only when I'm homesick, I go and eat weastern food.

连词"只有"后边常有"才"呼应，先说出条件，后说出结果。而"只有"表示的条件是唯一的，别的条件都不行。如：

The conjunction "只有" is often collocated with "才"。At first a condition is mentioned, then the result. However the condition expressed with "只有" is exclusive, it is impossible for any other conditions to produce the mentioned result.

（1）只有多听多说，才能学好汉语。

（2）只有尊重别人，别人才尊重你。

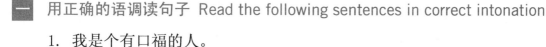

练习 • Exercises

一　用正确的语调读句子 Read the following sentences in correct intonation

1. 我是个有口福的人。

2. 请朋友们来聚聚，吃顿饭吧？

3. 我建议来个自助餐。

4. 谁爱吃什么就取什么。

5. 我早上起得晚，还不太饿。

6. 我真羡慕你，吃什么都长不胖。有口福啊！

7. 要是真想瘦一点儿，最好的办法是运动。

8. 谢谢！我不会喝酒。

9. 我只能少来一点儿。

10. 尝尝不同风味的菜，感觉真好。

二 替换句中画线部分的词语

Substitute the underlined parts in the sentences

1. 我建议来个自助餐。

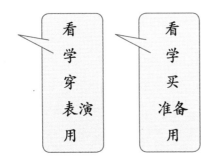

大家都学普通话
我们喝葡萄酒
去做客的人都带一个菜
有女朋友的都带女朋友来
谁猜错了，谁喝一杯酒

2. 谁爱吃什么就取什么。

看
学
穿
表演
用

看
学
买
准备
用

3. 你别笑话我，这几个月我又长了好几斤，越来越胖了。

我的声调不太准
我还是不明白你的意思
我不会用筷子
我不太了解你们的文化
我的汉语不太好

4. 自己觉得舒服比什么都强。

身体健康
真心相爱
上网聊天儿
玩儿
不上课

重要
幸福
轻松
快乐
高兴

5. 要是真想瘦一点儿，　　　　　　最好　的办法是运动。

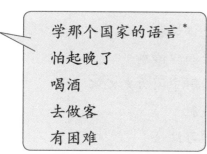

学那个国家的语言＊
怕起晚了
喝酒
去做客
有困难

到那个国家去
请闹钟帮忙
喝葡萄酒
带点小礼物
找朋友帮忙

6. （运动）一停下来，　　　　　　（身体）会更胖。

不注意
夸他
有声音
刮风
说错

感冒
他
我
天气
心情

厉害
开心
睡不着觉
冷
紧张

7. 他们不一定　　　　　　非　让你喝不可。

学语言
想减肥
写好汉字
老不吃早饭
要学好汉语

多听多说
天天运动
坚持多写
影响健康
来中国

8. 如果我是你，我就说："谢谢！我不会喝酒。"

不喝这么多酒。
不原谅他。
受不了。
接受＊他的建议。
不跟他吵架。

9. 这 _____ 对 我了解中国很有好处。

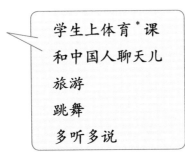

学生上体育*课
和中国人聊天儿
旅游
跳舞
多听多说

身体健康
提高口语水平
了解中国历史文化
减肥
学习汉语

10. 只有想家的时候， 我才 _____ 去吃一顿西餐。

做自己喜欢的事
考完了试
周围安静
你陪她去
星期天

特别有兴趣
会感到轻松
能睡着
放心
有时间

三 填上适当的量词

Fill in the brackets with proper measure words

1. 朋友们要来咱们家，我想请他们吃（   ）饭。咱们来个自助餐怎么样？先准备一（   ）凉菜，等大家都来了再做几（   ）热菜。酒得好好儿准备，除了来（   ）葡萄酒，再来（   ）啤酒什么的。

2. 早晨喝（   ）豆浆，吃两（   ）油条，或者吃一（   ）面条儿，又便宜又方便，真不错。有时候吃（   ）面包，一（   ）鸡蛋，再来（   ）咖啡，也挺好。

四 体会下面各句中"点"的不同含义

Learn the different meanings of "点" in the following sentences

1. 我一点儿也不喜欢这种味道。
2. 八点了，怎么还不上课？
3. 便宜点儿吧。
4. 我很喜欢中餐，可是有点儿不习惯用筷子。
5. 你想吃什么菜，就点什么菜好了。
6. 汉语考了八十点五分。

五 对话表演 Perform the dialogue

甲： 才一个月没见，你怎么又胖了？

乙： 没办法，连喝水都长肉。

甲： 我想你一定有四种特别的习惯。

乙： 哪四种习惯？

甲： tāng táng tǎng tàng!

乙： 什么？

甲： 汤糖躺烫，"汤"就是喝汤，"糖"就是喜欢吃甜的，"躺"就是喜欢睡觉，"烫" 就是喜欢吃特别热的东西。

乙： 我从来没这么总结*过，好像真是这么回事。

六 说一说 Have a talk

1. 你每天吃早饭吗？吃早饭时，你有什么特别的习惯？
2. 你喜欢怎么请客？
3. 你觉得减肥的好办法是什么？
4. 你怎么看"有口福"？你是不是一个"有口福"的人？

七 成段表达 Narration

1. 我的饮食习惯。
2. 我们国家跟中国在饮食习惯上的不同。
3. 健康比什么都重要。

八 说一说，笑一笑 Talk and laugh

改错

"你每天晚上只喝两杯白酒，今天怎么要了四杯？"

"我自己觉得喝两杯已经够了，可我老婆还不满意。"

"她怎么不满意？"

"每天晚上我一到家，她总是对我说：'你看你，又喝个半醉！'"

Correct Mistakes

A: You drink two glasses of distilled spirit every day. Why should you ordered four today?

B: I thought two glasses was enough, but my wife wasn't satisfied!

A: How?

B: Every night when I go back home, she always says to me, Look at you! You've got half-drunk again!

Chéngshì hǎo háishi nóngcūn hǎo?
城市 好 还是 农村 好?

（在家里）

儿　子：　咱们家也养只小动物吧。养只小狗好不好？

女　儿：　小狗跑跑跳跳的样子太可爱了，我也想养。

母　亲：　小狗是可爱，但是我反对你们养。在城市里养狗，有很多麻烦事。

儿　子：　不养狗，养只猫吧。

女　儿：　我想养只白猫，有一对蓝眼睛的白猫。我天天给它洗澡。

儿　子：　我天天喂它饭。妈妈，您不反对了吧？

母　亲：　我还得问问你们的爸爸是什么意见。

（经理回答顾客的问题）

经　理：　您想买房子吗？

顾　客：　想看看这里的新房子。

经　理：　您请这边看。有两间一套的，有三间一套的。

顾　客：　三间一套的有几个卫生间？

经　理：　有的一个，有的两个。

顾　客：　客厅大不大？

经　理：　挺大的。

顾　客：　这里在农村和城市之间，环境很好。交通呢？

经　理：　有好几路公共汽车都到这里。

顾　客：　孩子上学方便吗？

经　理：　您看，中学在那儿，小学在这儿，都很近。

顾　客：　价钱怎么样？

经　理：　比市中心的房子便宜三分之一左右。买一套吧？

顾　客：　我先回家商量商量再做决定。

（在家里）

哥　哥：　我真不明白，别人都想办法往城市里搬，你却非要回农村的老家去。这到底是怎么回事？

弟　弟：　我喜欢农村生活，喜欢大自然和那里的农民。咱们的老家，环境优美，空气新鲜。天蓝蓝的，山绿绿的，马啊、牛啊、羊啊在草地上吃草，像一幅画儿似的，要多美有多美。

哥　哥：　可是农村的生活条件哪比得上城市呢？有好多不方便的地方。

弟　弟：　那是以前，在农村劳动和生活都很苦。现在变化可大了。不信，你

去农村看看，那里不一定比城市差。而且，工业、交通等对城市的污染越来越严重了，对健康一点儿好处也没有。

（弟弟说）

　　城市好还是农村好？这不是一句话就能说清楚的。城市里人太多、太挤了，哪有农村舒服呢？说实话，刚到农村的时候，我也觉得这不习惯、那不方便的。可经济在发展、社会在进步，农业生产搞得越来越好，农民都富起来了，城市和农村的差别越来越小。在农村住的时间越长，我对农村的感情越深。

注　释　Notes

1. 在城市里养狗，有很多麻烦事

There are a lot of troubles if you keep a dog in the city.

　　为了保护城市环境和市民的安全、健康，城市的有关部门对养狗有许多管理法规和条例，如登记户口、打狂犬疫苗等等，这些就是课文中所谓的"麻烦事"。

In order to protect the environment of the city and to ensure the safety and health of the citizens, the relative departments of the city's government make many regulations and statutes for keeping dogs, such as registering residence, taking hydrophobia vaccine and so on, which are called "麻烦事" in the text.

2. 别人都想办法往城市里搬，你却非要回农村的老家去。

Other people are all thinking of ways of moving to the city, but you would rather move to the countryside.

副词"却"表示转折，语气较轻。只能用在主语后、动词前。如：

The adverb "却" expresses a transition, the tone is softer. It can only be used after the subject and before the verb. For example:

（1）小猫、小狗可爱极了，爸爸、妈妈却反对我们家养。

（2）城市的污染越来越严重，农村的风景却像画儿似的，要多美有多美。

3. 这到底是怎么回事？

What's really going on here?

副词"到底"用在疑问句或表示疑问的结构里，追究事物的真相。有时是选择式问句，有时后面有疑问词。如：

The adverb "到底" is used in an interrogative sentence or in the interrogative form to seek the truth. It is sometimes used in an alternative interrogative sentence, at times is followed by a question word. For example:

（1）我也不清楚，到底是我说错了，还是他听错了。

（2）你想过没有？到底为什么会这样？

4. 马啊、牛啊、羊啊在地上吃草，像一幅画儿似的，要多美有多美。

Cows and sheep are on the meadow eating grass, and it's like a painting, it's hard to describe how beautiful it is.

助词"似的"跟"像、好像"等连用，或表示比喻，或表示情况相似。如：

Auxillary word "似的" is sometimes written "是的", and is used together with the conjunctions "像、好像". It is used either to express a metaphor or to refer to the similarity of situations. For example:

（1）她把宿舍布置得像家似的。

（2）我这个朋友像老师似的，教会了我许多东西。

5. 像一幅画似的，要多美有多美。

It looks like a picture, and is as beautiful as you can imagine.

"要多 A 有多 A"是个口语中常用的表示夸张的格式，意思是 A 的程度极高，高得没有限制。"要多美有多美"的意思是说美极了，太美了，美得无法形容。再如：

"要多 A 有多 A" is a pattern frequently used in the colloquial language to express exaggeration, meaning the level of A is so high that it can not be limited. "要多美有多美" means extremely beautiful, beyond description. Other examples:

（1）这个孩子要多可爱有多可爱。

（2）早上坐地铁，要多挤有多挤。

6. 城市里污染越来越严重了，对健康一点儿好处也没有。

The pollution in the city is more and more serious, and it's not good for health at all.

在这里"一点儿好处也没有"就是"没有一点儿好处"的意思。"一点儿"和"也"结合，之后再用否定副词"不"或"没"，表示最大程度的否定。如：

Here "一点儿好处也没有" means "没有一点儿好处" (It's not good at all.) "一点儿" is used together with "也", followed by a negative adverb "不" or "没", indicating negation to the greatest extent. For example:

（1）对不起，今天我一点儿时间也没有。

（2）刚来中国的时候，我一点儿汉语也不会说。

"一点儿"还可以和"都"结合。如：

"一点儿" can also work together with "都". For example:

（1）昨天晚上出去玩儿了，一点儿觉都没睡。

（2）她一点儿钱都不乱花。

7. 刚到农村的时候，我也觉得这不习惯、那不方便的。

I also found it is hard to get used to or it is very inconvenient when I came to the countryside at first.

句中的"这"是"这方面"，"那"是"那方面"，总起来表示"很多方面"。"这"和"那"的后面都用否定副词"不"或"没"，否定副词之后的动词或形容词可以是相同的，也可以是不同的。如：

"这" means "这方面" in the text, and "那" means "那方面", together they indicate "很多方面" (many aspects). "这" and "那" are both followed by a negative adverb "不" or "没", and the verb or adjective after the adverbs can be either the same or different. For example:

（1）到了一个新环境，肯定是这不了解那不熟悉的。

（2）明天就考试了，我还这没复习、那没复习呢。

练 习 Exercises

一 用正确的语调读句子 Read the following sentences in correct intonation

1. 咱们家也养只小动物吧。养只小狗好不好？

2. 在城市里养狗，有很多麻烦事。

3. 不养狗，养只猫吧。

4. 您不反对了吧？

5. 我还得问问你们的爸爸是什么意见。

6. 您看，中学在那儿，小学在这儿，都很近。

7. 像一幅画儿似的，要多美有多美。

8. 农村的生活条件哪儿比得上城市呢？

9. 那是以前，现在变化可大了。

10. 城市好还是农村好？这不是一句话就能说清楚的。

二 替换句中画线部分的词语

Substitute the underlined parts in the sentences

1. <u>小狗</u>　是　<u>可爱</u>，但是　<u>我反对你们养</u>。

环境	不错	交通不太方便
她	漂亮	我不喜欢她
聚会	没意思	又不好意思离开
价钱	很贵	质量确实非常好
旅游	辛苦	收获也很大

2. 不养<u>狗</u>，　<u>养只猫</u>吧。

吃鸡	吃鱼
住城市	住农村
听新闻	听音乐
喝啤酒	喝可乐
坐汽车	坐地铁*

3. <u>您请这边看。</u>　有　<u>两间一套的</u>，　有　<u>三间一套的</u>。

我的朋友	学文学	学历史
留学生	住学校里	住学校外
同学中	在城市长大	在农村长大
您可以多看看	贵	便宜
我们的宿舍	一个人一间	两个人一间

4. 我真不明白，别人都想办法往城市里搬，你却非要去农村。

> 他为什么不同意大家的意见
>
> 别人都坐飞机，你却要坐火车
>
> 抽烟有什么好处
>
> 你为什么不爱他了
>
> 有些年轻人为什么不同意老年人再婚

5. 像一幅画儿似的， 要多美 有多 美。

> 夜里肚子疼
> 菜太辣了
> 有的汉字
> 地铁里
> 去医院

> 难受
> 辣
> 难写
> 挤
> 麻烦

> 难受
> 辣
> 难写
> 挤
> 麻烦

6. 农村的生活条件哪比得上城市呢？ 有好多不方便的地方。

> 饭馆
> 我
> 新同学
> 我
> 租房子住

> 家里
> 他
> 老同学
> 你
> 买房子住

> 地方不干净
> 不如他的地方
> 不熟悉的情况
> 不顺利的事
> 不自由的地方

7. 那里 不一定比 城市差。

> 出租车
> 明天天气
> 贵的菜
> 他
> 我知道的

> 地铁快
> 今天好
> 便宜的菜好吃
> 你年龄大
> 你多

8. （城市里的污染）对健康一点儿 　　 好处也没有。

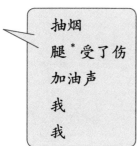

抽烟
腿*受了伤
加油声
我
我

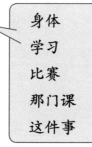

身体
学习
比赛
那门课
这件事

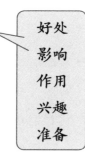

好处
影响
作用
兴趣
准备

9. 城市里人太多、太挤了，哪有农村舒服呢？

住学校外边
我
我们国家
我的汉语
我想的

住学校宿舍方便
人家安妮漂亮
中国这么多人
你说得好
这么麻烦

10. 我也觉得 　　 这不 习惯、那不 方便的。

开始我总是
别对我总是
女朋友老说我的房间
我也知道自己的发音*
你问他什么，他都是

喜欢
放心
干净
标准*
了解

满意
放心
整齐*
正确*
知道

11. 在农村住的时间 　 越 　 长， 　 我对农村的感情 　 越 　 深。

抽烟
年龄
在中国住的时间
妈妈对孩子照顾
教育水平

多
大
长
周到
高

对身体
对生活的理解
对中国的了解
孩子的生活能力
经济发展

不好
深
广泛
差
快

三 读例句，体会加点词语的意思并模仿对话

Read the examples, make sure of the meanings of the dotted words and then perform the dialogues

1. 甲：在城市里养狗，有很多麻烦事。

   乙：不养狗，养只猫吧。您不反对了吧？

   甲：我还得问问你们的爸爸是什么意见。

2. 甲：价钱怎么样？

   乙：比市中心的房子便宜三分之一左右。买一套吧？

   甲：我回家商量商量再做决定。

3. 甲：农村的生活条件哪比得上城市呢？有好多不方便的地方。

   乙：那是以前，现在变化可大了。

4. 甲：你老家的环境好吗？

   乙：可好了，环境美得像一幅画儿似的。

四 根据课文内容回答问题

Answer the questions according to the content of the text

1. 母亲对养小动物是什么态度？为什么？
2. 新房子怎么样？
3. 弟弟为什么喜欢农村？
4. 哥哥和弟弟对农村的看法有什么不同？

五 辩论 Debate

1. 甲方：养动物有好处。

   乙方：养动物没有好处。

   Side A: There is benefit in keeping animals.

   Side B: There isn't any benefit in keeping animals.

2. 甲方：城市比农村好。

   乙方：农村比城市好。

   Side A: City is better than countryside.

   Side B: Countryside is better than city.

参考句式： Sentence patterns for reference:

我反对……	那还不如……	不一定比……差
还是……好	越……越……	……是……，但是……
比得上		

六 小演讲 Mini speech

1. 我和小动物
2. 我爱我的城市
3. 我的老家在农村

七 说一说，笑一笑 Talk and laugh

学语言就是要多听

上法文课时，老师完全用法文讲，学生不能完全听懂。学生要求老师加一点儿中文。老师解释*说："不要怕听不懂，学语言就是要多听。你们每天听我说法文，时间长了，自然就明白了。"这时，有个学生忽然说："可是我每天听小狗叫，也不明白它的意思。"

You must listen more when you learn a foreign language

In French class, the teacher taught in French and the students couldn't get all that he said. Being asked by the students to add some Chinese in his teaching, the teacher explained, "Don't be afraid of not getting what I said. You must listen more when you learn a language. If you listen to my French everyday, you will surely understand what I said after some time." Suddenly, a student said, "But I don't think I can understand what my dog is saying even I hear it barking everyday!"

Zhēn wèi nǐ gāoxìng
真 为 你 高 兴

（在校园里）

陈 红： 王丽，听说你要出国留学了。

王 丽： 我刚申请，八字还没一撇呢。

陈 红： 出国留学都要办什么手续？

王 丽： 先考英语，比如 TOFEL、GRE、IELTS 什么的。成绩好才能申请到奖学金。

陈 红： 英语你准没问题。大家不是都叫你"活词典"吗？好像没有你不知道的词。

王 丽： 哪里，这次我没考 IELTS，只考了 TOEFL 和 GRE，成绩还没出来。我发了几封申请书，一封回复的邮件都没收到。

陈 红： 如果有了录取通知书，手续就简单了吧？

王 丽： 不清楚。我只知道办护照要好几个工作日，办签证还要面谈什么的。

（在王丽家）

陈 红： 学校的录取通知书来了！

王 丽： 真的？快给我看看。

陈 红： 通知书怎么说？

王 丽： 是全额奖学金！

陈 红： 什么时候开学？

王 丽： 八月二十六号。

陈 红： 住的地方怎么安排？

王 丽： 学校里有宿舍，也可以自己在校外租房子。为了更快地提高语言水平，

学校要求外国学生第一年必须住在当地人家里。

陈 红： 有道理。王丽，祝贺你！真为你高兴。

王 丽： 谢谢！是你给我带来了好消息，我得好好儿谢谢你。

（王丽说）

我已经来到美国，成了一名硕士研究生。办手续时，我遇到了许多麻烦事。现在，把我的经验跟你们说说：

申请美国硕士研究生，要求大学平均成绩八十分以上，还需要 TOEFL 八十分以上或者 IELTS 6.5 分以上的成绩。

申请奖学金，一般来说，需要 GRE 成绩。另外，还要提供推荐信、发表过的论文、研究成果、社会实践证明什么的。

（陈红说）

俗话说："人各有志。"王丽出国留学了，我真为她高兴。她是每年几十万出国学习的中国人中的一个。不过，我真的不想出国学习。原因很多，例如，我出国后，谁来照顾我母亲？还有，我的专业更适合在国内学。国内的条件越来越好，好的导师也越来越多，在国内学习同样能够成才。

注　释　Notes

1. 八字还没一撇呢

Nothing tangible is in sight yet.

"八"这个字一共两笔，一笔是撇，一笔是捺。写的时候，要先写撇，再写捺。"八字还没一撇"就是连一笔也没写，比喻事情根本还没有开始做呢，更别说完成了。

The Chinese character "八" has two strokes altogether, one is a left falling stroke, and the other is a right falling stroke. When writing, one must first write the left falling stroke, and then the right falling stroke. "八字还没一撇" means that one stroke hasn't even been written yet, indicating that the thing hasn't started at all, it is a long way to talk about all accomplishment.

2. 活词典

a walking dictionary

比喻记忆力特别好、懂得的事特别多、了解的情况特别广的人，就像词典一样，问他什么他都知道。

This metaphor refers to a person whose memory is particularly good, who knows a lot and is clear about information on many aspects, just like a dictionary, and whatever you ask, he will know.

3. 要求大学平均成绩八十分以上。

You must have an undergradnate mean score of eighty and above.

在这里"以上"表示比前边说的那个数目更多。如：

The numeral "以上" expresses an amount larger than the number previously mentioned.

（1）韩国学生在一半以上。

（2）他每门课都在九十分以上。

4. 人各有志

这句俗话的意思是各人有各人的志向，言外之意就是人的志向不同，不必强求一律。

This proverb means that each one has his own ideal. The implication is that different people have different dreams and there is not necessarily all the same.

5. 原因很多，例如，我出国后，谁来照顾我母亲？

There many reasons, for instance, who will take care of my mother if I go abroad?

"例如"是举例用语，放在所举的例子前面。如：

"例如" is a term used for listing examples, it is placed in front of the examples listed.

（1）人各有志，例如，有人希望当翻译，有人希望做教师。

（2）出国前先考英语，例如，TOEFL，IELTS 什么的。

练习 Exercises

一　用正确的语调读句子 Read the following sentences in correct intonation

1. 听说你要出国留学了。

2. 我刚申请，八字还没一撇呢。

3. 出国留学都需要办什么手续？

4. 英语你准没问题。

5. 祝贺你！真为你高兴。

6. 谢谢！是你给我带来了好消息。

7. 我得好好儿谢谢你！

8. 把我的经验跟你们说说。

二　看一看，说一说，哪句话符合课文原意

Read and talk about the following sentences, which one is accordant to the original meaning of the text

1. 王丽的出国申请还没寄出去。

2. 出国手续办起来不简单。

3. 王丽出国后应该在校外租房子。

三　替换句中画线部分的词语

Substitute the underlined parts in the sentences

1. 我刚<u>申请</u>，八字还<u>没一撇</u>呢。

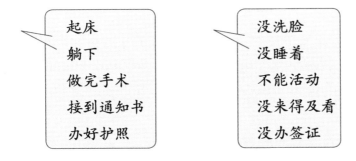

起床	没洗脸
躺下	没睡着
做完手术	不能活动
接到通知书	没来得及看
办好护照	没办签证

2. <u>成绩好</u>　　　　才能<u>申请到奖学金</u>。

睡得早	起得早
多运动	身体好
基础好	提高得快
有护照	办签证
申请到奖学金	有条件去学习

3. 好像没有你<u>不认识</u>的词。

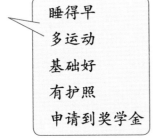

| 不知道的事 |
| 不爱好的运动 |
| 没去过的地方 |
| 不了解的情况* |
| 不感兴趣的问题 |

4. 　我发了几封申请书，一封回复的邮件　　　　都没收到。

我等了半天	个人	没来
我看了看	句话	不懂
天很晴	片云	没有
太远了	点儿	看不清楚
他走了几个月	点儿消息	没有

5. 　为了更快地提高语言水平，学校要求外国学生第一年必须住在当地人家里。

写出漂亮的汉字，老师	我们天天练习
不污染环境，公司	办公室里不准吸烟
多一些机会，学校	毕业生*多参加几个公司的面试
安全，妻子	当司机的丈夫遵守交通规则
治好他的病，大夫	病人必须做手术

6. 　王丽出国留学了，　　我　真为她高兴。

你要迟到了，	我	为你着急
她还没回来	我	替她担心
你自己去吧，	我	不感兴趣
加油！	我们	希望你赢
常回家看看，	父母	想你们

7. 　原因很多，　　　　例如，　　我出国后，谁来照顾我母亲？

名胜古迹	香山*、长城*我都去过。
我准备的水果	苹果、葡萄、橘子什么的。
有名的大学	北京大学、清华大学*等都是。
服装的颜色	红的、白的、蓝的都好看。
年轻人的理想	出国留学、自己开公司，都挺不错的。

8．在国内学习　　　　　　同样能够成才。

旅游
买东西
跳舞
在旅行车上睡觉
用手机

可以学习汉语
能练口语
能锻炼身体
可以休息
能够上网

四　读例句，体会加点词语的意思并模仿对话

Read the examples, learn the meanings of the dotted words and perform the dialogues

1．甲：大家不是都叫你"活词典"吗？考试你准没问题。

　　乙：哪里，这次我考得也不太好。

2．甲：为了更快地提高语言水平，学校要求外国学生第一年必须住在当地人家里。

　　乙：有道理。

五　根据第一二两段对话，介绍一下有关王丽出国的事

Describe the matter about Wang Li's going abroad according to Dialogue 1 and 2

提示：王丽的英语很好，她已经申请出国留学……她给国外的大学寄了几份申请……

　　　一天，她收到了学校的通知书……

六　你办留学手续时，遇到过什么麻烦事？介绍一下你的经验。

七　说一说 Have a talk

你对在国内学习和出国留学有什么看法？你是怎么选择的？为什么？

八　说一说，笑一笑 Talk and laugh

重新做人 *

一个爱喝酒的丈夫对妻子说："从明天开始，我要重新做人。"第二天晚上，他又是喝得大醉回家。妻子说："我以为你要重新做人，就再也不喝酒了。"丈夫说："没想到我重新做的这个人也爱喝酒。"

Becoming a new person

A husband who was always keeping the alcohol bottle told his wife, "From tomorrow on, I'll reform myself and become a new person!" But the following night when he came back home he was still plastered. The wife said angrily, "I thought you wouldn't drink anymore since you wanted to reform yourself!" The husband answered, "I also didn't expect that this new "I" also like drinking!"

第十六课 为友谊干杯！

Wèi yǒuyì gān bēi!

（学生们在告别晚会上）

甲： 你怎么才来？晚会早就开始了。

乙： 对不起，让大家久等了。我把时间看错了。

丙： 罚酒一杯！

乙： 我不爱喝啤酒，来杯葡萄酒吧。

丁： 好，人都齐了。现在让我们举杯，首先为咱们在中国成了好朋友，干杯！

乙： 还要预祝咱们早日再见面，干杯！

丙： 时间像流水一样，几年的留学生活一下子就过去了。

丁： 是啊，咱们刚来学院的情景，好像就发生在昨天似的。

甲： 还记得吗？当时你穿一件黄上衣，他穿着灰毛衣，她留着长长的直发……

乙： 那时候，你分不清我们俩，经常叫错我们的名字。

甲： 你呢？上课回答问题的时候，你说的错句子出了不少笑话。

丙：　人家现在说得跟中国人一样流利了。

乙：　哪里，还差得远，差得远。

丁：　我建议：咱们每一个人，用自己国家的语言说一句"为友谊干杯！"

甲：　这个建议有意思。来，一、二、三！

众：　为友谊干杯！

丁：　我还有个建议，咱们在这儿照张合影吧。

（在宿舍）

山　下：　彼得，行李都收拾好了吗？

彼　得：　收拾好了。要离开了，还真舍不得。分别以后，不知道什么时候才

　　　　　能再见面。

山　下：　别难过，我相信咱们一定有再见面的机会。几点的飞机？

彼　得：　十二点的，应该提前两个小时到机场。

山　下：　有人送你去机场吗？

彼　得：　有，他们说在楼下集合。

山　下：　九点了，该下去了吧？

彼　得：　该走了。再见，我的房间！再见，我的床！

山　下：　我拿行李，送你上车。

（留学生们送彼得到机场）

甲：　　飞机就要起飞了，快上去吧。

彼 得： 真舍不得离开你们哪！以后可别忘了我。

乙： 怎么会呢？常跟我们联系吧。

彼 得： 有机会去我们国家的话，一定要跟我联系。

丙： 别忘了寄一张你和夫人在婚礼上的照片来。

彼 得： 好，记住了。

丁： 一路平安！

甲： 替我们问候你的父母！

彼 得： 谢谢，再见！

众： 再见！

（彼得说）

　　我在中国的留学生活结束了，我又高兴又难过。高兴的是：学到了真正的汉语，交了许多朋友，游览了许多名胜古迹，对中国的过去和现在更了解了。难过的是：我真舍不得离开中国，舍不得离开我的学校、我亲爱的老师和同学们。我有一个愿望：回国后，我要继续提高汉语水平，关心中国各方面的情况，好更广泛地了解中国。

注　释　Notes

1. 让大家久等了

keeping all of you waiting for a long time

"让大家久等了"这句话是迟到的人客气地向等待自己的人表示歉意。"久"是时间长的意思。

"让大家久等了" is a sentence used by a guest who has come late to politely express his regret to the people waiting for him. "久" means a long time.

2. 罚酒一杯

Fine him a glass of wine!

指惩罚的方式是让被惩罚的人当众喝下一杯酒。

This means that the way of punishment is to make the punished person drink a glass of wine in public.

3. 几年的留学生活一下子就过去了。

Several years of study abroad life goes by in an instant.

副词"一下子"也可以说成"一下"，表示某种动作发生、完成得快，或某种现象出现得突然。"一下子"后边常有"就"。如：

（1）刚才还是大晴天，一下子就下起雨来了。

（2）听你这么说，我一下子就明白了。

4. 一定要跟我联系

Make sure you will keep in touch with me!

这句话表示说话人希望对方一定要跟他接上关系，保持关系。"联系"既可用作动词，是彼此接上或保持关系的意思；也可用作名词，是指彼此之间的联络。如：

This sentence indicates that the speaker hopes the other party could contact him/her and they can keep in touch with each other. "联系" can be used as a verb, meaning get in touch with or keep in touch with each other, and it can also be used as a noun, referring to the contact between each other. For example:

（1）为准备聚会，我已经联系了二十多位同学了。

（2）请一定给我回信，好继续咱们之间的联系。

5. 一路平安！

Have a good trip!

送别远道的朋友或亲人时常说的祝词，希望远行的人路上一切顺利，平安到达目的地。

差不多的意思还可以说"一路顺风"。

Friends or family who see people off often say this well-wishing phrase in the hope that everything goes smoothly for people traveling far and that they arrive safely and peacefully at their destination. "一路顺风" is also used to express such meaning.

 练习 Exercises

一 用正确的语调读句子 Read the following sentences in correct intonation

1. 为友谊干杯！
2. 对不起，让大家久等了。
3. 我把时间看错了。
4. 时间像流水一样。
5. 不知道什么时候才能再见面。
6. 我拿行李，送你上车。
7. 真舍不得离开你们哪！
8. 有机会去我们国家的话，一定要跟我联系。
9. 一路平安！
10. 替我们问候你的父母！

二 替换句中画线部分的词语

Substitute the underlined parts in the sentences

1. 对不起，让大家久等了。

> 您为我担心
> 你们辛苦
> 你白劳动
> 你受苦
> 您感到不痛快

2. 我　　　　　　把 时间看错了。

他	聚会的事忘了
我总	这件事记在心里
我们留学生	宿舍当做家
我们都	手续办好了
大家都	你当做好朋友

3. 我　不爱　　　　喝啤酒，　来　杯葡萄酒吧。

他	吃葡萄	个香蕉
老人	听流行歌曲	支*民歌*
南方人	吃咸的	点儿甜的
你	穿红的	件黄的
我	看报纸	本杂志*

4. 现在让我们举杯，为咱们在中国成为好朋友，干杯！

这次相聚*
我们的友谊
丽莎的生日
老师们的健康
我们合作愉快

5. 几年的留学生活一下子就过去了！

抽烟的习惯	改掉
美好*的愿望	实现
新同学和老同学	熟悉
太阳一出来，天	晴
躺下以后	睡着

6. 还记得吗？当时 你穿一件黄上衣，他穿着灰毛衣……

> 我们还以为她是你夫人呢。
>
> 大家都为你干了杯。
>
> 他连一句普通话也不会说。
>
> 你忘了带钱包。
>
> 我们用汉语表演节目。

7. 飞机就要 起飞了，快 上去吧。

学校	开学	准备准备吧
咱们	分别	照张合影吧
晚会	开始	进去吧
学习	结束	抓紧时间找工作吧
天	下雨	回去吧

8. 有机会去我们国家的话，一定要跟我联系。

打算去别人家做客	先约好时间
有病有事不能上课	跟老师请假
学习有困难	跟老师说
离开宿舍	把门锁*好
口语不流利	多说多练

9. 替我们问候你的父母！

> 我们问候你的夫人。
>
> 我谢谢他。
>
> 我通知他。
>
> 我表示感谢。
>
> 我照顾一下行李。

10. 我在中国的留学生活结束了。

> 热闹的婚礼
> 足球比赛
> 留学的生活
> 毕业晚会
> 他的演讲

三 读例句，体会加点词语的意思并模仿对话

Read the examples, learn the meanings of the dotted words and then perform the dialogues

1. 甲： 你怎么才来？晚会早就开始了。
   乙： 对不起，让大家久等了。

2. 甲： 真舍不得离开你们哪！以后可别忘了我。
   乙： 怎么会呢？常跟我们联系吧。

3. 甲： 别忘了寄一张你和夫人在婚礼上的照片来。
   乙： 好，记住了。

四 根据课文回答问题

Answer the questions according to the text

1. 大家为什么罚学生乙喝酒？他为什么来晚了？
2. 干杯时大家说了哪些话？
3. 学生们刚认识时有什么有意思的事？
4. 彼得回国以前的感觉怎么样？
5. 彼得在中国的留学生活怎么样？

五 根据情景设计对话 Design dialogues according to the following situations

为朋友送别

1. 在告别晚会上
2. 在飞机场

参考句式：	别难过	一路平安	舍不得
	还记得……	为……干杯	别忘了……

六 成段表达 Narration

1. 我的留学生活结束了。

2. 再见，我的朋友们！

七 实践：在毕业联欢会上说一段话 Practice: Give a speech in the graduation party

参考词语 Words for reference

> 结束　难过　交……朋友　了解　收获　舍不得　希望　继续　联系　合影

七 说一说，笑一笑 Talk and laugh

让耳朵也高兴

甲：你知道人们在干杯前为什么要碰杯*吗？

乙：互相祝贺嘛。不对吗？

甲：因为喝酒时，眼睛能看到酒的颜色，鼻子能闻*到酒的香气*，嘴能尝到酒的味道，只有耳朵没事做，不高兴。一碰杯，杯子发出的声音，耳朵听到了，也高兴起来。

To make the ears happy

A: Do you know why people clink their glasses before they drink toast?

B: It's only cheers, isn't it?

A: Well, because when you drink a wine, your eyes can see the color of the wine, your nose can smell the scent and your tongue can taste its flavour. Only the ears are unhappy since they have nothing to do. When people clink their glasses the ears can hear and be happy!

你知道吗？ Do You Know？ (4)

节日与历法

喜欢过节是人们共同的情趣。一年十二个月，几乎月月有节日。在中国，比较大的节日有：

	公历	农历
元旦	1月1日	
春节		正月初一
元宵节		正月十五
妇女节	3月8日	

清明节	4 月 5 日	
劳动节	5 月 1 日	
端午节		五月初五
儿童节	6 月 1 日	
中秋节		八月十五
重阳节		九月初九
国庆节	10 月 1 日	

　　上表所列节日的时间，有的用公历表示，有的用农历表示。公历是阳历的一种，为国际通用的纪年法，以地球绕太阳一周的时间（365.24219 天）为一年，平年 365 天，闰年 366 天。一年分十二个月，一般大月每月 31 天，小月每月 30 天。农历是中国的传统历法，相传创始于夏代，所以叫夏历，也叫旧历，通称阴历，距今已有四千多年的历史了。农历以月亮绕地球一周的时间（29.3059 天）为一个月，大月每月 30 天，小月每月 29 天，积十二个月为一年。一年 354 天或 355 天，平均每年的天数比公历约少 11 天。所以农历中有的年份设置了闰月，有闰月的年份全年 383 或者 384 天。现在在中国公历和农历同时并用，中国的传统节日都用农历来表示。

　　中国的传统节日一般都有来历，过节时也有一定的讲究。比如：春节在这些节日里，是最大最热闹的节日，它是中国的新年。过春节时，家家都要吃饺子，亲戚朋友相互拜年，说："过年好""春节好"等吉祥话，还要放鞭炮、贴对联等。元宵节也叫灯节，那天讲究吃元宵、看花灯。端午节人们都吃粽子，不少地方还有赛龙舟活动。中秋节是团圆的节日，人们要和家人团聚，赏月、吃月饼。重阳节是敬老和登高的节日，年轻人这一天都要去看望长辈，祝他们健康长寿。还有不少人纷纷走出家门，去登高、爬山、观赏菊花。

　　你想了解中国人在过这些节日时的传统风俗习惯吗？那么你不妨走进普通中国人的家里去看一看。

Holidays and Calendars

Enjoying holidays is the common emotional appeal for people. There are holidays in nearly each of the twelve months. In China, the relatively important holidays are:

	Solar Calendar	Lunar Calendar
New Year's	Jan. 1st	
Spring Festival		1st Month, 1st Day
Lantern Festival		1st Month, 15th Day
Women's Day	Mar. 8th	
Qingming Festival	Apr. 5th	

Labor Day	May 1st	
Dragon Boat Festival		5th Month, 5th Day
Children's Day	June 1st	
Mid-Autumn Festival		8th Month, 15th Day
Double-Ninth Festival		9th Month, 9th Day
National Day	Oct.1st	

Some of the dates of the holidays in the table above are shown in the solar calendar and some are shown in the lunar calendar. The solar calendar is the commonly used international chronology, which takes one of Earth's orbits around the Sun (365.24219 days) as a year; regular years have 365 days, bissextile years have 366 days, and a year is divided into twelve months. Generally, a "big month" has 31 days, and a "small month" has 30 days. The lunar calendar is the common ancient Chinese chronology, originated in the Xia dynasty, so it is called the "Xia calendar", and it is also called the "lunar calendar". It has a history of more than four thousand years. The lunar calendar takes the time of the Moon orbits around the Earth (29.3059 days) as a month, a "big month" has thirty days, and a "small month" has twenty-nine days, with a year consisting of twelve months. A year has 354 or 355 days, in average, there are eleven days less than in the solar calendar. So leap month was setted in lunar calendar, there are 383 days or 384 days in that years. Now in China both the solar calendar and the lunar calendar are used, and China's traditional holidays are all indicated in the lunar calendar.

All of China's traditional holidays have a origin, and there are sth particular about spending holidays. For example, Spring Festival is the biggest and most lively holiday, it is Chinese New Year. When celebrating Spring Festival, every family eats dumplings, friends and relatives all drop in on one another, saying auspicious words like, "Happy New Year!" and "Happy Spring Festival!", in addition to setting off firecrackers and pasting antithetical New Year's couplets. Yuanxiao Festival is also called the Lantern Festival, and on that day people eat sweet dumplings and watch the festive lanterns. On the Dragon Boat Festival people eat zongzi and there are dragon-boat racing activities in many places. The Mid-Autumn Festival is a time of gathering, people gather together with family members, appreciate the moon and eat mooncakes. The Double-Ninth Festival is a festival to respect the aged and climb mountains; on this day young people should pay a visit to their elders to wish them a long and healthy life, and many people leave their homes one after another to ascend heights, climb mountains, and appreciate chrysanthemums.

Would you like to understand the Chinese traditional custom and habits during these holidays? Then you shouldn't hesitate to visit an ordinary Chinese home to have a look.

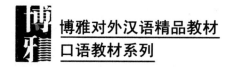

博雅对外汉语精品教材
口语教材系列

初级汉语口语(提高篇)

(第三版)

ELEMENTARY SPOKEN CHINESE (Improvement)
(Third Edition)

词语表与课文英文翻译

戴桂芙 刘立新 李海燕 编著

北京大学出版社
PEKING UNIVERSITY PRESS

目 录

分课词语表(英日韩文注释) ·· 1

  第 一 课　寒假过得很开心 ·· 1

  第 二 课　谁输谁赢还不一定呢! ·· 4

  第 三 课　麻烦您停一下儿车 ·· 7

  第 四 课　我从小就不爱吃鱼 ·· 10

  第 五 课　看把你高兴的 ·· 13

  第 六 课　对不起,我来晚了 ·· 15

  第 七 课　健康和快乐比什么都重要 ·· 19

  第 八 课　周末怎么过? ·· 22

  第 九 课　什么是真正的男女平等? ·· 25

  第 十 课　我是来找工作的 ·· 29

  第十一课　请你参加我们的婚礼 ·· 32

  第十二课　爱生活的人永远年轻 ·· 35

  第十三课　我是个有口福的人 ·· 38

  第十四课　城市好还是农村好? ·· 41

  第十五课　真为你高兴 ·· 45

  第十六课　为友谊干杯! ·· 48

词语总表 ·· 52

量词表 ·· 65

课文英文翻译 ·· 68

第一课　寒假过得很开心

◆ **生 词** New words

1. 开心　　　　（形）　　kāixīn　　　　feel happy, rejoice
楽しい
기분이 좋다

2. 金　　　　　（名）　　jīn　　　　　gold, a surname
金（きん）、ジン
금

3. 银　　　　　（名）　　yín　　　　　silver
銀
은

4. 幸福　　　　（形）　　xìngfú　　　happy, happiness
幸福である、幸せである
행복하다

5. 福　　　　　（名）　　fú　　　　　luck, good fortune
福（ふく）、フー
복

6. 另外　　　　（代）　　lìngwài　　　in addition, besides
別の
그밖의

7. 关照　　　　（动）　　guānzhào　　to take care of, to keep an eye on
面倒を見る、世話をする
돌봐주다

8. 好听　　　　（形）　　hǎotīng　　　pleasant to hear
聞いて気持ちがよい、美しい
듣기 좋다

9. 下边　　　　（名）　　xiàbian　　　under, below
次
다음

10. 接着　　　　（动）　　jiēzhe　　　to carry on, to follow
続いて、引き続いて
계속하다

11. 华裔　　　　（名）　　huáyì　　　Chinese descendant
外国国籍の中国系住民
해외에 거주하는 중국인 후손; 화교

12. 行李	（名）	xíngli	luggage
			荷物
			짐
13. 家乡	（名）	jiāxiāng	hometown
			故郷、郷里
			고향
14. 特产	（名）	tèchǎn	specialty
			特産
			특산물
15. 向	（介）	xiàng	towards, in the direction of
			～に
			…를 향하여
16. 问好		wèn hǎo	to say hello to, regards
			よろしく言う
			안부하다
17. 碰见		pèng jiàn	to run into, to come across, to meet
			（おもいがけなく）出くわす、出会う
			우연히 만나다
18. 聚	（动）	jù	to get together
			集まる
			모이다
19. 聚会	（动、名）	jùhuì	to get-together; social gathering
			集まり
			모임, 집회
20. 假期	（名）	jiàqī	vacation, holiday
			休暇、休みの間
			방학(휴가) 기간
21. 当	（动）	dāng	to be, to act as
			～になる、担当する
			…이 되다
22. 辛苦	（形）	xīnkǔ	hard working
			苦労する
			고생하다
23. 有意思		yǒu yìsi	interesting
			面白い
			재미있다. 의미있다.
24. 爷爷	（名）	yéye	grandfather
			おじいさん(父方の)
			할아버지
25. 热闹	（形）	rènao	bustling with activity, lively
			にぎやかである
			벅적벅적하다, 번화하다

2

26. 小时候	（名）	xiǎo shíhou	in one's childhood
			小さいとき
			어릴 때
27. 出生	（动）	chūshēng	to be born
			生まれる
			출생하다
28. 感到	（动）	gǎndào	to feel
			感じる、思う
			느끼다
29. 亲切	（形）	qīnqiè	cordial, warm, kind
			親しい、心がこもっている
			친절하다
30. 变化	（动）	biànhuà	to change
			変わる、変化する
			변화하다

◆ 专名　Proper nouns

1. 金云福	Jīn Yúnfú	a name of Korean
		金雲福（人名）
		김운복(인명)
2. 山田有美	Shāntián Yǒuměi	a name of Japanese
		山田有美（人名）
		산전유미(인명)
3. 广东话	Guǎngdōnghuà	Guangdong dialect
		広東語
		광동어
4. 普通话	pǔtōnghuà	Mandarin
		標準語
		표준어
5. 吴平春	Wú Píngchūn	a name of Chinese
		呉平春（人名）
		우평춘(인명)

◆ 补充词语　Additional words

1. 感觉	（动）	gǎnjué	feel
			感覚・感じ
			느끼다, 여기다
2. 酒	（名）	jiǔ	liquor
			リキュール
			리큐어

3. 护士	（名）	hùshì	nurse 看護師 간호사
4. 国家	（名）	guójiā	country 国家 주
5. 情况	（名）	qíngkuàng	situation, case 情況 상황
6. 缺点	（名）	quēdiǎn	defect, shortcoming 欠点 약점

第二课　谁输谁赢还不一定呢！

◆生 词　New words

1. 输	（动）	shū	to lose 負ける 지다
2. 赢	（动）	yíng	to win 勝つ 이기다
3. 敲	（动）	qiāo	to knock たたく、たたいて音を立てる 두드리다; 노크
4. 邻居	（名）	línjū	neighbor 隣近所の人 이웃
5. 安静	（形）	ānjìng	to be quiet 静かにする 조용하다
6. 影响	（动）	yǐngxiǎng	to disturb, to affect, to influence 影響する、影響を及ぼす 영향을 주다
7. 喊	（动）	hǎn	to yell, to cry out 叫ぶ、わめく 큰 소리로 외치다
8. 叫	（动）	jiào	to shout 叫ぶ 부르다, 외치다

9. (几)比(几)	（动）	bǐ	to compare, compared to (得点が)～対～ (몇)대(몇)
10. 校园	（名）	xiàoyuán	campus キャンパス 교정. 캠퍼스
11. 足球	（名）	zúqiú	football サッカー 축구
12. (足球)场	（名）	chǎng	pitch (サッカーの)競技場 평탄한 공터 ,마당, 장
13. 队	（名）	duì	team チーム、隊 팀
14. 对	（动）	duì	to against ～対～である 서로 맞서다
15. 由(……组成)	（介）	yóu	from ～で、～によって …에 의하여, …로 부터
16. 组成	（动）	zǔchéng	form, make up (in to), compose 構成する、作り上げる、形作る 조직하다
17. 踢	（动）	tī	to kick 蹴る 차다
18. 比赛	（动）	bǐsài	to match, to contest, competition 試合をする 시합하다
19. 摔	（动）	shuāi	to trip 転ぶ 넘어지다
20. 站	（动）	zhàn	standing, to stand up 立(た)つ 서다
21. 推	（动）	tuī	to push 押す 밀다
22. 裁判	（名）	cáipàn	referee 審判・審判する 심판

23. 黄牌儿	（名）	huángpáir	yellow card イエローカード 옐로우 카드 (경고 카드)
24. 罚	（动）	fá	to punish 罰する、ペナルティー 벌하다
25. 进（球）	（名）	jìn	score（a goal） （球を）入れる 들어가다
26. 队长	（名）	duìzhǎng	captain, team leader キャプテン 주장
27. 队员	（名）	duìyuán	team member チームメンバー 팀 멤버
28. 进行	（动）	jìnxíng	to carry on, to execute 行う 진행하다
29. 拉拉队	（名）	lālāduì	cheerleading squad 応援団 응원단
30. 支持	（动）	zhīchí	to support 支持する 지지하다
31. 结束	（动）	jiéshù	to end, to finish 終わる 끝나다
32. 握手		wò shǒu	to shake hands 握手する 악수를 하다
33. 拥抱	（动）	yōngbào	to hug, to embrace 抱き合う 포옹하다

◆ 补充词语　Additional Words

| 1. 民族 | （名） | mínzú | nation, nationality 民族 민족 |
| 2. 夫妻 | （名） | fūqī | husband and wife 夫婦 부부 |

3. 门卫	（名）	ménwèi	guard
			ガード
			가드
4. 一切	（代）	yíqiè	everything
			あらゆる、すべての
			일체의, 온갖
5. 知识	（名）	zhīshi	knowledge
			知識
			지식
6. 网	（名）	wǎng	net
			ネット
			그물
7. 眼儿	（名）	yǎnr	mesh
			穴
			구멍
8. 合作	（动）	hézuò	to cooperate, to work together
			協力する
			합작

第三课　麻烦您停一下儿车

◆生词 New Words

1. 乘客	（名）	chéngkè	passenger
			乗客
			손님
2. 售票员	（名）	shòupiàoyuán	ticket seller
			切符を売る人、バスの車掌
			매표원, 차장
3. 反	（形）	fǎn	reverse
			反対、逆
			반대로, 거꾸로
4. 南边	（名）	nánbian	south
			南、南方
			남쪽
5. 北边	（名）	běibiān	north
			北、北方
			북쪽
6. 开(车)	（动）	kāi	to drive (a car)
			運転する、操縦する
			(차)를 운전하다

7. 对面	（名）	duìmiàn	opposite 対面、向かい 맞은편
8. 劳驾		láo jià	to excuse me, may I trouble you... すみません 죄송하지만
9. (车)站	（名）	zhàn	bus station 停留所・立つ 정류장
10. 准	（动）	zhǔn	to be accurate, exact 許可する ~할수있다
11. 出事		chū shì	to meet with an accident 事件が起こる 일이 일어나다
12. 闯	（动）	chuǎng	to run into, to force one's way in まっしぐらに突進する 마구 돌진하다, 휙 지나가다
13. 红灯	（名）	hóngdēng	red traffic light 赤信号 빨간 불
14. 伤	（动、名）	shāng	to hurt; injure 怪我をする、怪我 다치다
15. 上班		shàng bān	to go to work 会社に行く、通勤する 출근
16. 平安	（形）	píng'ān	safe and sound 無事である、平安である 평안
17. 遵守	（动）	zūnshǒu	comply with 従う 준수
18. 规则	（名）	guīzé	rule ルール 규칙
19. 新闻	（名）	xīnwén	news ニュース 신문
20. 市	（名）	shì	city 市 시

21. 起	（量）	qǐ	*measure word*
			件, 回
			건 (사건을 세는 단위)
22. 事故	（名）	shìgù	accident
			事故
			사고
23. 酒	（名）	jiǔ	liquor
			リキュール
			리큐어
24. 后	（名）	hòu	after
			後
			후
25. 结果	（连）	jiéguǒ	result
			結果
			결과
26. 重伤	（名）	zhòngshāng	serious injury
			重い
			심한
27. 轻伤	（名）	qīngshāng	slight wound
			軽い
			경한
28. 安全	（形）	ānquán	safe
			安全
			안전하다
29. 危险	（形）	wēixiǎn	dangerous, at risk
			危険である
			위험하다

◆ 补充词语　Additional Words

1. 零钱	（名）	língqián	small change
			小銭
			잔돈
2. 成绩	（名）	chéngjì	marks (of study), achievement
			成績
			성적, 성과
3. 奶奶	（名）	nǎinai	grandmother
			おばあちゃん
			할머니
4. 孙子	（名）	sūnzi	grandson
			孫
			손자

| 5. 到处 | （副） | dàochù | everywhere
至る所
어디나 |
| 6. 擦 | （动） | cā | to rub, to wipe
拭く
닦다, 문지르다 |

第四课　我从小就不爱吃鱼

◆ 生 词　New Words

1. 从小	（副）	cóngxiǎo	from childhood 小さいときから 어릴 때 부터
2. 餐厅	（名）	cāntīng	dinning room, restaurant レストラン 식당
3. 甲	（名）	jiǎ	be first, rank first 甲（順番をつけるときに用いる） 갑
4. 乙	（名）	yǐ	2nd of the 10 Heavenly Stems 乙（順番をつけるときに用いる） 을
5. 尖椒牛肉		jiānjiāo niúròu	stir-fried beef stirred with pepper ピーマンと牛肉の炒め物 고추 소고기 볶음
6. 炒蘑菇		chǎo mógu	fry mushroom きのこの炒め物 버섯 볶음
7. 蘑菇	（名）	mógu	mushroom きのこ, マッシュルーム 버섯
8. 丙	（名）	bǐng	3nd of the 10 Heavenly Stems 丙（順番をつけるときに用いる） 병
9. 不论……都……		búlùn……dōu……	no matter (what, how, etc.) たとえ〜であろうとも〜 …어떻든지
10. 也许	（副）	yěxǔ	maybe, probably もしかしたら〜かもしれない 아마

11. 营养	（名）	yíngyǎng	nutrition 栄養 영양
12. 丰富	（形）	fēngfù	rich, enrich 豊富である 풍부하다
13. 可乐	（名）	kělè	coke コーラ 콜라
14. 主食	（名）	zhǔshí	staple food 主食 주식
15. 渴	（形）	kě	thirsty のどが渇く 목마르다
16. 民族	（名）	mínzú	nation, nationality 民族 민족
17. 节日	（名）	jiérì	festival 記念日、節句、祭日 경축일, 기념일
18. 龙(船)	（名）	lóng	dragon 竜 용
19. 粽子	（名）	zòngzi	a pyramid-shaped dumpling ちまき 종자(단오날 먹는 음식)
20. 举行	（动）	jǔxíng	to hold (a meeting, etc.) 行う、挙行する 거행하다
21. 奶奶	（名）	nǎinai	grandmother おばあちゃん(父方の) 할머니
22. 外卖	（名）	wàimài	take out テイクアウトする 배달 음식
23. 排队		pái duì	to line up 列に並ぶ、順番を待つ 줄을 서다
24. 不久	（形）	bùjiǔ	soon, before long まもなく 오래지 않아, 곧

25. 路过	（动）	lùguò	to pass, to go past 通りかかる、通る (…곳을)거치다, 통과하다
26. 牌子	（名）	páizi	sign, plate 掲示板 팻말
27. 上面	（名）	shàngmiàn	above 上 위.위쪽
28. 老板	（名）	lǎobǎn	boss 経営者、店主 사장, 상관
29. 不但	（连）	búdàn	not only... but also ～ばかりでなく …할 뿐만 아니라
30. ……得很		……déhěn	very とても（程度の高いことを表す） 정도가 심한 것을 나타냄
31. 十分	（副）	shífēn	very, extremely 十分に、非常に 대단히
32. 想念	（动）	xiǎngniàn	to think of, to miss 懐かしむ、恋しがる 생각하다

◆ 专名　Proper Nouns

| 1. 端午节 | | Duānwǔ Jié | the Dragon Boat festival
旧暦の5月5日　端午の節句
단오절 |
| 2. 龙船节 | | Lóngchuán Jié | the Dragon Boat festival
竜船レースを競う
용선절 |

◆ 补充词语　Additional Words

| 1. 困难 | （名） | kùnnan | difficulty
困難
곤란함 |
| 2. 食品 | （名） | shípǐn | foodstuff
食品
식품 |

3. 题目 　　　（名）　　　tímù　　　　subject, topic
テーマ
제목

第五课　看把你高兴的

◆生词　New Words

1. 消息　　　（名）　　　xiāoxi　　　news, information
知らせ、ニュース
소식

2. 成绩　　　（名）　　　chéngjì　　　result, achievement
成績
성적

3. 语文　　　（名）　　　yǔwén　　　（spoken and written) language
日本の『国語』科に相当する
국어

4. 数学　　　（名）　　　shùxué　　　mathematics
数学
수학

5. 外语　　　（名）　　　wàiyǔ　　　foreign language
外国語
외국어

6. 名　　　　（量）　　　míng　　　（measure word for persons)
位（席次を表す量詞)
명 (사람을 세는 단위)

7. 表扬　　　（动）　　　biǎoyáng　　to praise
ほめる
칭찬

8. 除了……以外　（连）　chúle……yǐwài　aside from, except for
…を除いて
~을 빼고는, ~을 제외하고

9. 方面　　　（名）　　　fāngmiàn　　side (of an issue)
方面
방면·부분·분야

10. 落后　　　（形）　　　luòhòu　　　fall behind
遅れる、後れをとる
떨어지다, 낙후되다

11. 合唱　　　（名）　　　héchàng　　chorus
合唱（する)
합창

13

12. 选	（动）	xuǎn	to choose
			選挙
			선거

13. 班长	（名）	bānzhǎng	captain
			班長　学級委員長
			제목

14. 课外	（名）	kèwài	after school
			課外、授業以外
			과외

15. 活动	（动、名）	huódòng	to move about activity; activity
			活動
			활동하다

16. 组	（名）	zǔ	group
			組、グループ
			조, 팀

17. 按照	（介）	ànzhào	according to
			～によって
			로, …에 따라

18. 兴趣	（名）	xìngqù	interesting
			興味
			흥미

19. 报名		bào míng	to enter one's name, to sign up
			申し込む、応募する
			신청하다

20. 声音	（名）	shēngyīn	voice
			声
			소리.목소리

21. 方法	（名）	fāngfǎ	method
			方法
			방법

22. 发声		fā shēng	produce a sound
			発声
			발성하다. 발음하다.

23. 歌手	（名）	gēshǒu	singer
			歌手
			가수

24. 实现	（动）	shíxiàn	to realize, to come true
			実現する
			실현되다, 이루어지다

25. 梦想	（名）	mèngxiǎng	dream
			夢、切望
			꿈

1. 凉快	（形）	liángkuai	cool 涼しい 시원하다. 서늘하다
2. 痛快	（形）	tòngkuai	joyful, delighted 思いっきり、心ゆくまで 통쾌하다, 시원하다
3. 表示	（动）	biǎoshì	to show 示す、表す 표시하다
4. 甲方	（名）	jiǎfāng	party A 甲方 갑이라는 쪽
5. 乙方	（名）	yǐfāng	party B 乙方 을이라는 쪽
6. 过程	（名）	guòchéng	process 過程 과정
7 傻	（形）	shǎ	silly, stupid 頭が悪い 어리석다. 우둔하다.
8 难道	（副）	nándào	(used to reiterate a rhetorical question)

第六课　对不起，我来晚了

◆ 生 词　New Words

1. (手)表	（名）	biǎo	watch (腕)時計 손목 시계
2. 下班		xià bān	to get off work 仕事を終える 퇴근
3. 复印	（动）	fùyìn	to copy, photocopy コピーする 복사하다

4. 份	（量）	fèn	*measure word* 部（新聞や書類を数える量詞） 복사자료, 신문, 문건등을 세는 단위
5. 速度	（名）	sùdù	speed 速度 속도
6. 总(是)	（副）	zǒng	always いつも 항상
7. 理由	（名）	lǐyóu	reason 理由 이유
8. 原谅	（动）	yuánliàng	forgive, pardon 許す 용서하다
9. 约会	（名）	yuēhuì	to have a date 〜したいと思う 희망하다
10. 有的是		yǒudeshì	have plenty of, no lack of たくさんある 얼마든지 있다. 아주 많이 있다.
11. 愿意	（动）	yuànyì	would like, to be willing 〜したいと思う 희망하다
12. 心事	（名）	xīnshì	weight on one's mind, worry 心配事 걱정거리, 마음의 근심
13. 有些	（代）	yǒuxiē	some, somewhat 少し、多少 조금
14. 另	（形）	lìng	another 〜のために …를 위하여
15. 文化	（名）	wénhuà	culture, civilization 文化 문화
16. 选择	（动）	xuǎnzé	to choose 選択する、選ぶ 선택하다
17. 国界	（名）	guójiè	border, national boundary 国境 국경

18. 真心	（名）	zhēnxīn	wholehearted 本心、偽りのない心 진심
19. 相爱	（动）	xiāng'ài	to love each other 互いに思い合う 서로 사랑하다
20. 不同	（形）	bùtóng	different 同じでない 같지 않다
21. 管	（动）	guǎn	to have charge of しつける 관리하다
22. 正（因为）	（副）	zhèng	just まさに、まさしく (…이기 때문에)
23. 明白	（动、形）	míngbai	to understand; clear 分かる、理解する 이해하다
24. 爱人	（名）	àirén	husband or wife 恋人、配偶者 남편 혹은 아내
25. 满分	（名）	mǎnfēn	full marks 満点 만점
26. 想法	（名）	xiǎngfǎ	idea 考え、考え方 방법
27. 尊重	（动）	zūnzhòng	to respect 尊重する、大事にする 존중하다
28. 受（教育）	（动）	shòu	to get 受ける (교육)을 받다
29. 教育	（动、名）	jiàoyù	to educate 教育 교육
30. 心	（名）	xīn	heart 心 마음
31. 性格	（名）	xìnggé	character 性格 성격

32. 周围	（名）	zhōuwéi	surrounding, circumstances 周り、周囲 주위
33. 夸	（动）	kuā	to praise 大げさに言う、誇張する 과장하다
34. 确实	（副）	quèshí	indeed 確かに 확실히

◆ 补充词语　Additional Words

1. 填	（动）	tián	fill （表を）埋める 기입하다. 써 넣다.
2. 表(格)	（名）	biǎo	table フォーム 양식
3. 步	（名）	bù	step 歩 걸음
4. 活	（动）	huó	to live 生きる 살다
5. 妻管严	（名）	qīguǎnyán	hen-pecked 恐妻家 공처가
6. 金钱	（名）	jīnqián	money 金銭 금전
7. 家和万事兴		jiā hé wàn shì xīng	a peaceful family will prosper 家庭円満であれば、何ごともスムーズに運ぶ 가화만사성. 집안이 화목하면 모든 일이 잘 된다.
8. 可爱	（形）	kě'ài	cute, lovely かわいい 귀엽다, 사랑스럽다
9. 墨镜	（名）	mòjìng	sunglasses サングラス 선글라스

10. 修理	（动）	xiūlǐ	to repair
			修理する
			수리하다

第七课　健康和快乐比什么都重要

◆ 生 词　New Words

1. 跳舞		tiào wǔ	to dance
			ダンスをする
			춤을 추다

2. 傍晚	（名）	bàngwǎn	toward evening, at dust
			夕方
			저녁, 밤

3. 红红绿绿		hónghóng lǜlǜ	colorful
			色とりどりで鮮やかなさま
			울긋 불긋하다

4. 练（书法）	（动）	liàn	to practise (calligraphy)
			書道を習う
			를 연습하다

5. 儿女	（名）	érnǚ	son and daughter, children
			息子と娘; 子供
			자녀

6. 带（孩子）	（动）	dài	to bring/take care (of the children)
			（子供を）つれる
			데리고 다니다

7. 老	（形）	lǎo	old
			年を取る
			늙다

8. 可怕	（形）	kěpà	scared, fearful
			恐ろしい
			두렵다

9. 旅游	（动）	lǚyóu	to travel
			観光する、旅行する
			여행하다

10. 羡慕	（动）	xiànmù	admire, envy
			うらやましい
			부러워하다

11. 并（不）	（副）	bìng(bù)	(used before a negative for emphasis)
			決して～でない
			결코…하지 않다

12. 养老院	（名）	yǎnglǎoyuàn	nursing home 老人ホーム, 養老院 양로원
13. 感动	（动）	gǎndòng	to be moved 感動する、心を打たれる 감동하다
14. 好多	（数）	hǎoduō	a lot たくさんの 많은
15. 反对	（动）	fǎnduì	to oppose, to be against 反対する 반대하다
16. 自杀	（动）	zìshā	to suicide 自殺する 자살하다
17. 理解	（动）	lǐjiě	to understand, to comprehend 理解する 이해하다
18. 商量	（动）	shāngliang	to discuss 相談する 의논하다
19. 人家	（代）	rénjia	other people ほかの人、他人、人様 사람들
20. 伯伯	（名）	bóbo	uncle おじさん 큰아버지; (아저씨)
21. 照顾	（动）	zhàogù	to take care 世話を焼く 돌보다
22. 考虑	（动）	kǎolǜ	to think over, to consider 考える、考慮する 고려하다
23. 代替	（动）	dàitì	to substitute わる、代わりを務める 대신하다
24. 再婚	（动）	zàihūn	to be remarried 再婚する 재혼하다
25. 自由	（名、形）	zìyóu	freedom; free 自由である 자유

26. 存	（动）	cún	to store, to keep, to preserve
			保存する、預かる、預ける
			보관하다, 맡기다

27. 银行	（名）	yínháng	bank
			銀行
			은행

28. 怎样	（代）	zěnyàng	how about, what about
			どのように
			어떻게

29. （掉）光	（形）	guāng	nothing left, all gone
			抜け落ちる
			빠지

30. 这些	（代）	zhèxiē	these
			これら
			이런 것들, 이러한

31. 剩（下）	（动）	shèng	to leave behind, remaining
			残る
			남다

32. 捐	（动）	juān	to donate
			寄付する
			기증하다

33. 穷	（形）	qióng	poor
			貧しい
			가난한

34. 有用		yǒu yòng	useful
			有用である、役に立つ
			필요하다, 쓸모있다

◆ 补充词语　Additional Words

1. 面试	（动）	miànshì	to have an interview
			面接
			면접시험 하다

2. 笑话	（名）	xiàohua	joke
			笑い話
			재미있는 말

3. 难过	（形）	nánguò	to feel sad
			悲しい
			힘들다

4. 舍不得		shěbude	to be loath to part with or give up
			使うこと・捨てることを惜しむ
			아쉽다

5. 爱情	（名）	àiqíng	love 愛情 애정
6. 基础	（名）	jīchǔ	foundation 基礎 기준
7. 补习	（动）	bǔxí	to take a make-up course 補習する 보습하다
8. 教授	（名）	jiàoshòu	professor 教授 교수
9. 夫人	（名）	fūrén	Mrs., madam 夫人 부인
10. 收养	（动）	shōuyǎng	to adopt 他人の子供を引き取って育てる 입양하다

第八课　周末怎么过？

◆ 生词　New Words

1. 周五	（名）	zhōuwǔ	Friday 金曜日 금요일
2. 同事	（名）	tóngshì	colleague 同僚 직장 동료
3. 收拾	（动）	shōushi	to sort, to tidy, to put in order 片づけをする 청소하다
4. 饭桌	（名）	fànzhuō	dinner table 食卓、テーブル 밥상
5. 不好意思		bù hǎo yìsi	to be sorry, to be shy 恥ずかしい 부끄럽다.죄송합니다.실례합니다.
6. （看不）惯	（形）	guàn	cannot bear the sign of, not used to 目障りである、気に食わない 익숙되지 않다, 눈에 거슬리다

7. 老年	（名）	lǎonián	elderly 高齢者 노인
8. 之间	（名）	zhījiān	between 間に 사이
9. 代沟	（名）	dàigōu	generation gap ジェネレーションギャップ 대리 구매 하다
10. 待	（动）	dāi	to stay （どこへも出かけないで）じっとしている 머무르다
11. 过去	（名）	guòqù	past 過去 과거
12. 经历	（名）	jīnglì	experience, to go through 経験、体験 경험
13. 书本	（名）	shūběn	book 本、書物 책, 서적
14. 收获	（名）	shōuhuò	harvest 得るところ、収穫 소득
15. 洗（衣服）	（动）	xǐ	to wash (clothes) （服を）洗う （옷을) 씻다, 빨다
16. 洗衣机	（名）	xǐyījī	washing machine 洗濯機 세탁기
17. 费	（动）	fèi	to cost (a lot) 費やす、かかる 쓰다, 소비하다
18. 只好	（副）	zhǐhǎo	have to 〜するほかない 할 수 없이
19. 千万	（副）	qiānwàn	by all means, absolutely どんなことがあっても、くれぐれも 부디, 제발
20. 要不	（连）	yàobù	or または 또는

21. 周一	（名）	zhōuyī	Monday 月曜日 월요일
22. 附近	（名）	fùjìn	nearby 近所、付近 근처
23. 商场	（名）	shāngchǎng	department store マーケット、デパート 백화점
24. 团聚	（动）	tuánjù	to get together, reunion 集まる、団欒する 모이다
25. （一周）来	（助）	lái	up to the present （一週間）以来 한 주간 정도의
26. 钓（鱼）	（动）	diào	to go fishing 魚釣り 낚시하다
27. 培养	（动）	péiyǎng	to cultivate, to nurture 育成する、育て上げる 배양하다
28. 利用	（动）	lìyòng	to use, to utilize 利用する 이용하다
29. 各（种）	（代）	gè(zhǒng)	every 各種の、さまざまな 각종
30. 展览	（名）	zhǎnlǎn	exhibit, show 展覧 전람
31. 痛快	（形）	tòngkuai	joyful, delighted 思いっきり、心ゆくまで 통쾌하다, 시원하다

◆ 补充词语　Additional Words

| 1. 回忆 | （动） | huíyì | to recall
思い出す
기억하다 |
| 2. 家务 | （名） | jiāwù | household duties
家事
집안 일 |

3. 做法	（名）	zuòfǎ	method of work やり方 (하는)방법
4. 吹牛		chuī niú	boast 誇る 자랑
5. 一生	（名）	yìshēng	whole life 一生 일생
6. 卧室	（名）	wòshì	bedroom 寝室 침실
7. 地下	（名）	dìxià	underground 地下 지하
8. 盒子	（名）	hézi	box, case （小型の）容器 작은 상자. 곽
9. 纸条	（名）	zhǐtiáo	paper slip/note 書きつけ 종이 쪽지. 메모지

第九课　什么是真正的男女平等？

◆ 生词　New Words

1. 真正	（形）	zhēnzhèng	genuine, true 正真正銘の、真の 정말, 진짜
2. 平等	（形）	píngděng	equal 平等である 평등
3. 沙发	（名）	shāfā	sofa ソファー 소파
4. 抽(烟)	（动）	chōu	to smoke (cigarette) 吸う 피다
5. (干)活儿	（名）	huór	work 仕事をする、働く (일을) 하다

6. 气	（动）	qì	to be angry, engaged	
			怒る	
			화나다	
7. 批评	（动）	pīpíng	to criticize	
			しかる	
			비평하다	
8. 社会	（名）	shèhuì	society	
			社会	
			사회	
9. 模范	（名）	mófàn	role model	
			模範、手本	
			모범	
10. 改变	（动）	gǎibiàn	to change	
			変える	
			변하다	
11. 认错		rèn cuò	to admit wrongdoing	
			過ちを認める	
			잘못을 인정하다	
12. 今后	（名）	jīnhòu	from now on	
			今後	
			오늘 이후	
13. 家务	（名）	jiāwù	household chores	
			家事	
			집안일.가사	
14. 劝（架）	（名）	quàn	to mediate	
			介在する	
			중재	
15. 表现	（动）	biǎoxiàn	to show	
			態度・表現する、表す	
			표현하다	
16. 演讲	（动）	yǎnjiǎng	to present, speech	
			演説する、講演する、弁論する	
			강연하다	
17. 题目	（名）	tímù	title, topic	
			タイトル、テーマ	
			제목	
18. 复杂	（形）	fùzá	complicated, complex	
			複雑である	
			복잡하다	
19. 到处	（副）	dàochù	everywhere	
			いたるところ、あちこち、方々	
			어디나	

20. 连……也……		lián……yě……	even...also …でさえも… ~조차도~하다.심지어~하다
21. 认为	（动）	rènwéi	to think 〜と考える、〜と思う …로 알다, 여기다
22. 男人	（名）	nánrén	man 男性 남자
23. 特点	（名）	tèdiǎn	distinguishing feature 特徴 장점
24. 女人	（名）	nǚrén	woman 女性 여자
25. 讨论	（动）	tǎolùn	to discuss 議論 토론
26. 话题	（名）	huàtí	topic, subject 話題 화제
27. 既……也……	（连）	jì……yě……	both...and 〜の上に〜だ、〜でもあれば〜でもある …할 뿐만 아니라 …하다
28. 政治	（名）	zhèngzhì	politics 政治 정치
29. 经济	（名）	jīngjì	economics 経済 경제
30. 现代	（名）	xiàndài	modern 現代 현대
31. 打(基础)	（动）	dǎ	to establish (基礎を)固める (기초를) 닦다
32. 目前	（名）	mùqián	at present, at the moment 現在 목전에, 눈앞에
33. 存在	（动）	cúnzài	to exist 存在する 현존하다

34. 现象	（名）	xiànxiàng	appearance 現象 현상
35. 嫁	（动）	jià	to marry (a man) 嫁に行く、嫁ぐ 시집가다
36. 算	（动）	suàn	to be considered …とみなす 계산에 넣다.치다
37. 处理	（动）	chǔlǐ	deal with 扱う 처리

◆ 补充词语　Additional Words

1. 演讲稿	（名）	yǎnjiǎnggǎo	speeches スピーチ 연설
2. 恋爱	（动）	liàn'ài	in love 恋愛 데이트하다
3. 能力	（名）	nénglì	ability 能力 능력
4. 原因	（名）	yuányīn	reason 理由 이유
5. 现实	（名）	xiànshí	reality 現実 현실
6. 玻璃	（名）	bōli	glasses ガラス 유리
7. 亲爱的		qīn'àide	dear 親しい人に対する呼びかけ 친애하는
8. 却	（副）	què	but ところが 오히려, 반대로

第十课　我是来找工作的

◆ 生 词　New Words

1. 职员	（名）	zhíyuán	office worker, staff member 職員 직원
2. 纸	（名）	zhǐ	paper 紙 종이
3. 笔	（名）	bǐ	(tool for writing and drawing) 鉛筆、ボールペンなどの筆記用具 펜
4. 经理	（名）	jīnglǐ	manager 支配人、経営者 경리
5. 秘书	（名）	mìshū	secretary 秘書 비서
6. 报纸	（名）	bàozhǐ	newspaper 新聞 신문
7. 贵(公司)	（形）	guì	esteemed (company) 貴(社) 귀사
8. 客人	（名）	kèrén	guest 客 손님
9. 参观	（动）	cānguān	to visit 見学する、参観する 참관하다
10. 简历	（名）	jiǎnlì	resume 略歴 간략한 경력
11. 证明	（名）	zhèngmíng	evidence, certificate 証明(書) 증명
12. 毕业证	（名）	bìyèzhèng	certificate of graduation 卒業証明書 졸업증

13. (复印)件	(名)	jiàn	(copied) document
			(コピー) 文書
			복사본. 문서.서류.문건.
14. 面试	(动)	miànshì	to interview
			面接する
			면접 시험
15. 领导	(名)	lǐngdǎo	leader
			指導者
			사장님
16. 发展	(动)	fāzhǎn	to develop, to expand
			発展する
			발전하다
17. 前途	(名)	qiántú	future prospect
			前途、将来性
			장래
18. 能力	(名)	nénglì	ability, faculty
			能力
			능력
19. 技术	(名)	jìshù	skill, technology
			技術
			기술
20. 增加	(动)	zēngjiā	to increase, to add
			増加する、増える
			증가하다
21. 收入	(名)	shōurù	income
			収入
			수입
22. 通知	(动)	tōngzhī	to notice
			知らせる、連絡する・通知、知らせ
			알리다, 통보하다
23. 招	(动)	zhāo	to recruit, to enroll
			募集する
			모집하다
24. 其中	(代)	qízhōng	among, in
			その中
			그 중에
25. 不少		bù shǎo	many
			多くの
			많은
26. 中年	(名)	zhōngnián	middle age
			中年
			중년

27. 印象	（名）	yìnxiàng	impression
			印象
			인상
28. 年龄	（名）	niánlíng	age
			年齢
			연령
29. 熟悉	（动）	shúxī	to know well, to be familiar with
			よく知っている、熟知する
			잘 알다, 훤하다
30. 负责	（动、形）	fùzé	to be in charge of; responsible
			責任感がある、着実でまじめである
			책임지다

◆ **专名** Proper Nouns

1. 李林		Lǐ Lín	a Chinese name
			李林(人名)
			이림(인명)
2. 刘山		Liú Shān	Liu Shan
			劉山(人名)
			유산(인명)

◆ **补充词语** Additional Words

1. 背	（动）	bèn	to memorize (a text)
			暗記する
			외우다
2. 及格		jí gé	to pass (an exam)
			合格する
			합격하다
3. 林肯		Línkěn	Mr. Lincoln
			リンカーン(人名)
			링컨(인명)
4. 总统	（名）	zǒngtǒng	president
			大統領
			대통령
5. 勇气	（名）	yǒngqì	courage
			勇気
			용기
6. 请求	（名）	qǐngqiú	requisition
			リクエスト
			요청

7. 老婆	（名）	lǎopo	wife
			妻
			부인

第十一课　请你参加我们的婚礼

◆ 生 词　New Words

1. 婚礼	（名）	hūnlǐ	wedding
			結婚式
			혼례
2. 喜糖	（名）	xǐtáng	wedding candy
			婚礼の時に配る祝いのあめ
			결혼 사탕
3. 喜事	（名）	xǐshì	happy wedding
			祝い事
			혼사
4. 喜酒	（名）	xǐjiǔ	wedding wine
			結婚の祝いの酒
			결혼 술
5. 新娘	（名）	xīnniáng	bride
			花嫁
			신부
6. 怪不得		guàibude	no wonder
			道理で～だ
			어쩐지
7. 新郎	（名）	xīnláng	groom
			新郎
			신랑
8. 浪漫	（形）	làngmàn	romantic
			ロマンチック
			낭만적이다
9. 恋人	（名）	liànrén	lover
			恋人
			연인
10. 日子	（名）	rìzi	day, days
			日にち、日取り
			날짜
11. 顺	（形）	shùn	smooth
			順調である、円滑である
			순조롭다

12. 宴会	（名）	yànhuì	banquet 宴会、パーティー 연회
13. 主婚人	（名）	zhǔhūnrén	person who presides over a wedding ceremony 婚礼の主催者 주례
14. 举（杯）	（动）	jǔ	to raise one's glass (to propose a toast) グラスを持ち上げる (잔)을 들어 올리다
15. 干杯		gān bēi	to cheer 乾杯する 건배
16. 拜	（动）	bài	to salute, to make courtesy call 挨拶する 절하다
17. 恋爱	（动）	liàn'ài	in love 恋愛する 연애
18. 经过	（名、动）	jīngguò	process; to experience 経緯、いきさつ・通過する、通る 경과
19. 行	（动）	xíng	can あなたができる 당신은할수있습니다
20. 补充	（动）	bǔchōng	to replenish, supplement 補足する、追加する 보충하다
21. 同班		tóng bān	to be in the same class クラスメート 같은 반
22. 突然	（形）	tūrán	suddenly 突然 갑자기
23. 故事	（名）	gùshi	story ストーリー 스토리
24. 精彩	（形）	jīngcǎi	wonderful すばらしい 근사하다, 훌륭하다
25. 和美	（形）	héměi	harmonious and happy むつまじく楽しい 사이가 좋다, 정답다

26. 白头	（名）	báitóu	old age
			白髪
			흰머리

27. 上（百）	（动）	shàng	over (hundred), more than
			達する
			백명이 넘는다는 의미

28. 新人	（名）	xīnrén	new couple
			新郎新婦
			신랑과 신부

29. 主持	（动）	zhǔchí	to preside
			司る
			집행(하다)

30. 广泛	（形）	guǎngfàn	extensive, wide
			幅広い
			폭넓다

31. 天生	（形）	tiānshēng	inborn, innate
			生まれつきの
			천성적

32. 占	（动）	zhàn	to occupy
			占める
			차지하다, 점령하다

33. ……分之……		……fēnzhī……	fraction
			～分の～（分数やパーセントを表す）
			분지

34. 饭店	（名）	fàndiàn	hotel
			ホテル
			호텔

35. 意义	（名）	yìyì	meaning, sense, significance
			意味、意義
			의미

36. 说明	（动）	shuōmíng	to explain
			証明している
			설명(하다)

37. 婚姻	（名）	hūnyīn	marriage
			婚姻
			혼인

38. 重视	（动）	zhòngshì	to think highly of
			重視する
			중요하게 여기다

1. 农村	（名）	nóngcūn	countryside 農村 농촌
2. 套	（量）	tào	a set of そろい、一式(組になってるものを数える量詞) 세트
3. 退休		tuì xiū	to retire 退職する 은퇴하다
4. 祝福	（动）	zhùfú	to wish 祝福する 축복하다
5. 庆祝	（动）	qìngzhù	to celebrate 祝う 경축하다
6. 纪念日	（名）	jìniànrì	commemoration day, memorial day 記念日 기념일
7. 离婚		lí hūn	to divorce 離婚する 이혼(하다)

第十二课　爱生活的人永远年轻

◆ 生 词　New Words

1. ……来说		……láishuō	as... 〜といえば …로 말하면
2. 主要	（形）	zhǔyào	main, major 主に 대부분, 주로
3. 电视剧	（名）	diànshìjù	TV play テレビドラマ 텔레비젼극
4. 集	（量）	jí	volume, part 編(書籍、映画などを数える) 편 (연속극을 세는 단위)

5. 退休		tuì xiū	to retire 退職する 쉬다
6. 打(牌)	(动)	dǎ	to play (cards) (トランプを)する (도박을) 하다
7. 牌	(名)	pái	playing cards トランプ 도박이나 오락을 위한 기구
8. 麻将	(名)	májiàng	majiang マージャン 마작
9. 教师	(名)	jiàoshī	teacher 教師 교사
10. 备课		bèi kè	(of a teacher) to prepare the lessons 授業の準備をする 수업을 준비하다
11. 其他	(代)	qítā	other than, apart from 他の 기타
12. 歌迷	(名)	gēmí	music fan 歌を聴いたり歌ったりするのに夢中な人 노래 애호가
13. 下载	(动)	xiàzài	to download ダウンロード(する) 다운로드하다
14. 难道	(副)	nándào	*used to reiterate a rhetorical question* まさか〜ではあるまい、〜とでも言うのか 설마…하겠는가
15. 歌曲	(名)	gēqǔ	song 歌曲 노래, 가곡
16. 迷	(动)	mí	to be fascinated by, be crazy about ファン 팬(이다)
17. 奇怪	(形)	qíguài	odd, strange おかしい 이상하다
18. 相同	(形)	xiāngtóng	same 同じである 비슷하다

19. 厨房	（名）	chúfáng	kitchen
			台所
			부엌
20. 书房	（名）	shūfáng	study room
			書斎
			책방
21. 静	（形）	jìng	quiet
			静かである
			가만이 있다
22. 科学	（名、形）	kēxué	science; scientific
			科学
			과학
23. 晒	（动）	shài	(of the sun) to shine on
			日に当たる
			일광욕을 하다
24. 阳台	（名）	yángtái	balcony
			ベランダ
			베란다, 발코니
25. 篮球	（名）	lánqiú	basketball
			バスケットバール
			농구
26. 排球	（名）	páiqiú	volleyball
			バレーボール
			배구
27. 游览	（动）	yóulǎn	to browse
			遊覧する
			대충 훑어보다
28. 名胜	（名）	míngshèng	scenic spot
			名所
			명성
29. 古迹	（名）	gǔjì	historical relics
			旧跡
			고적
30. 导游	（名）	dǎoyóu	a tour guide
			ガイド
			여행 가이드
31. 律师	（名）	lǜshī	lawyer
			弁護士
			변호사
32. 中心	（名）	zhōngxīn	center
			センター
			센터

33. 健身	（动）	jiànshēn	fitness フィットネス 피트니스	
34. 实践	（动）	shíjiàn	to practise 実践する 실천(하다)	
35. 证明	（动）	zhèngmíng	to prove 証明する 증명하다	

◆ 补充词语　Additional Words

1. 历史	（名）	lìshǐ	history 歴史 역사	
2. 严	（形）	yán	strict 厳しい 엄격한	
3. 面条儿	（名）	miàntiáor	noodles 麺 국수	
4. 困	（形）	kùn	sleepy 眠い 졸리다	

第十三课　我是个有口福的人

◆ 生 词　New Words

1. 口福	（名）	kǒufú	gourmet's luck, the enjoyment of good foods ご馳走にありつく運 먹을 복	
2. 建议	（动）	jiànyì	to suggest, proposal 提案する、提案 제의하다, 건의하다	
3. 自助餐	（名）	zìzhùcān	buffet バイキングスタイル料理 부페	
4. 葡萄酒	（名）	pútaojiǔ	wine ワイン 와인	

5. 白酒	（名）	báijiǔ	white spirit バイチュウ（蒸留酒の総称） 백주, 소주
6. 醉	（动）	zuì	to be drunk 酔う 술 취하다
7. 主人	（名）	zhǔrén	host 主人 주인
8. 减肥		jiǎn féi	on diet ダイエットをする 다이어트
9. 笑话	（动）	xiàohua	to laugh at, ridicule 笑いものにする 비웃다, 놀리다
10. 身材	（名）	shēncái	figure, stature 体格、体つき、スタイル 몸매
11. 强	（形）	qiáng	strong, better よい、優れている 강하다, 세다
12. 坚持	（动）	jiānchí	to persist in, to insist on がんばって続ける 계속하다
13. 做客		zuò kè	to be guest 客となる 손님이 되다
14. 饮食	（名）	yǐnshí	food and beverage 飲食 음식
15. 中餐	（名）	zhōngcān	Chinese food 中華料理 중국 음식
16. 非……不可		fēi……bùkě	must, simply ～でなければならない …하지 않으면 안된다
17. 刀	（名）	dāo	knife ナイフ 나이프
18. 叉	（名）	chā	fork フォーク 포크

19. 左手	（名）	zuǒshǒu	left hand 左手 왼손
20. 右手	（名）	yòushǒu	right hand 右手 오른손
21. 切	（动）	qiē	to cut 切る 자르다
22. 鸡	（名）	jī	chicken にわとり 닭
23. 面条儿	（名）	miàntiáor	noodles めん 국수
24. 筷子	（名）	kuàizi	chopsticks 箸 젓가락
25. 面包	（名）	miànbāo	bread パン 빵
26. 冰箱	（名）	bīngxiāng	refrigerator 冷蔵庫 냉장고
27. 牛奶	（名）	niúnǎi	milk 牛乳 우유
28. 果汁	（名）	guǒzhī	juice 果汁、ジュース 과일쥬스
29. 豆浆	（名）	dòujiāng	soybean milk 豆乳 콩국
30. 油条	（名）	yóutiáo	deep-fried twisted dough sticks 揚げねじりパン 기름에 튀긴 꽈배기
31. 风味	（名）	fēngwèi	special flavor, local color 特色、味わい 맛
32. 感觉	（名、动）	gǎnjué	feeling; to feel ①感覚・感じ ②感じる ③…と思う 여기다

33. 好处	（名）	hǎochù	benefit
			有利な点、利益
			장점
34. 只有	（连）	zhǐyǒu	only
			～してこそ初めて～だ
			…해야만…이다
35. 西餐	（名）	xīcān	western food
			洋食
			양식

◆ 专 名　Proper Nouns

1. 麦当劳		Màidāngláo	**McDonald**
			マクドナルド
			맥도날드
2. 肯德基		Kěndéjī	**KFC**
			ケンタッキー
			켄터키 치킨

◆ 补充词语　Additional Words

1. 语言	（名）	yǔyán	language
			言語
			언어
2. 接受	（动）	jiēshòu	to get, to accept
			受け入れる
			받아드리다
3. 体育	（名）	tǐyù	sports
			体育
			체육
4. 总结	（动）	zǒngjié	to sum up
			まとめると
			요약하면

第十四课　城市好还是农村好?

◆ 生 词　New Words

1. 农村	（名）	nóngcūn	countryside, rural areas
			農村
			농촌

2. 养	（动）	yǎng	to raise	飼う 키우다, 기르다
3. 动物	（名）	dòngwù	animal	動物 동물
4. 狗	（名）	gǒu	dog	犬 개
5. 猫	（名）	māo	cat	猫 고양이
6. 喂	（动）	wèi	to feed	（動物に）えさを与える 먹이다
7. 意见	（名）	yìjiàn	suggestion, opinion	意見、異議 의견
8. 间	（量）	jiān	(measure for a room)	部屋を数える量詞 칸 (방을 세는 단위)
9. 套	（量）	tào	a set of	組になっているものを数える量詞 세트
10. 卫生间	（名）	wèishēngjiān	washing room, toilet	バスルームやトイレの総称 화장실
11. 客厅	（名）	kètīng	sitting room	客間、応接室 거실
12. 环境	（名）	huánjìng	environment	環境 환경
13. 路	（量）	lù	*measure for route*	路線、ルート 노선
14. 小学	（名）	xiǎoxué	primary school	小学校 초등학교
15. 决定	（名、动）	juédìng	decision; to decide	決める 결정

16. 却	（副）	què	but, yet, however
			〜のに、かえって
			오히려, 반대로
17. 到底	（副）	dàodǐ	in the end
			いったい
			도대체
18. 大自然	（名）	dàzìrán	nature
			大自然
			대자연
19. 农民	（名）	nóngmín	peasant, farmer
			農民
			농민
20. 优美	（形）	yōuměi	beautiful, graceful
			優美である
			우아하고 아름답다
21. 新鲜	（形）	xīnxiān	fresh
			新鮮である
			신선하다
22. 马	（名）	mǎ	horse
			馬
			말
23. 羊	（名）	yáng	sheep
			羊
			양
24. ……似的	（助）	…shìde	same as
			〜のようだ、〜みたいだ
			…와 같다
25. 劳动	（动）	láodòng	labour, work
			働く
			노동(하다)
26. 苦	（形）	kǔ	hard
			苦しい
			고생하다
27. 那里	（代）	nàlǐ	there
			そこ
			그곳
28. 工业	（名）	gōngyè	industry
			工業
			공업
29. 严重	（形）	yánzhòng	serious
			重大である、深刻である
			엄중하다

30. 挤	(动)	jǐ	to be crowded, to squeeze ぎっしり詰まる 붐비다, 꽉 차다
31. 农业	(名)	nóngyè	agriculture 農業(のうぎょう) 농업
32. 生产	(动)	shēngchǎn	to produce 生産する 생산하다
33. 差别	(名)	chābié	difference 隔たり、格差 차별, 차이
34. 感情	(名)	gǎnqíng	emotion, feelings 好感、愛着 감정

◆ 补充词语　Additional Words

1. 地铁	(名)	dìtiě	subway 地下鉄 지하철
2. 腿	(名)	tuǐ	leg 足 다리
3. 整齐	(形)	zhěngqí	neat, in good order きちんとしている 정연하다
4. 发音		fā yīn	to pronounce 発音 발음
5. 标准	(形)	biāozhǔn	standard 標準的である 표준적이다
6. 正确	(形)	zhèngquè	correct 正確である 정확하다
7. 解释	(动)	jiěshì	to explain 説明する 설명하다

44

第十五课　真为你高兴

1. 出国 　　　　　　chū guó
to go abroad
出国する、国を出る
출국

2. 申请 　　（动）　shēnqǐng
to apply for
申請する
신청하다

3. 撇 　　　（名）　piě
left-falling stroke
(漢字の筆画)左払い"ノ"
한자의 글자 중 삐치는 부분

4. 奖学金 　（名）　jiǎngxuéjīn
scholarship
奨学金
장학금

5. 活 　　　（形）　huó
alive, living
活きる
살다

6. 词典 　　（名）　cídiǎn
dictionary
字典、字引、辞書
자전

7. 申请书 　（名）　shēnqǐngshū
application form
申請書類
신청서

8. 回复 　　（动）　huífù
reply
返信する
답장하다.

9. 邮件 　　（名）　yóujiàn
e-mail
Eメール
이메일

10. 录取 　　（动）　lùqǔ
to be admitted (to a university or institution)
採用する
채용하다.고용하다

11. 通知书 　（名）　tōngzhīshū
notice letter
通知書類
통지서

12. 护照 　　（名）　hùzhào
passport
パスポート
여권

13. 工作日 　（名）　gōngzuòrì
work days
就労時間
근무일

14.	签证	（名）	qiānzhèng	visa
				ビザ
				비자
15.	面谈	（动）	miàntán	interview
				勇気
				용기
16.	全额	（名）	quán'é	full scholarship
				全額
				전액
17.	租	（动）	zū	to rent
				借りる
				세내다
18.	语言	（名）	yǔyán	language
				言葉、言語
				언어，말
19.	要求	（动）	yāoqiú	to require, to ask
				要求する
				요구하다
20.	必须	（副）	bìxū	must
				必ず～しなければならない
				꼭, 반드시
21.	当地	（名）	dāngdì	localiy
				現地、その土地
				현지
22.	硕士	（名）	shòushì	master's degree
				修士
				면담하다. 직접 만나서 이야기하다
23.	遇到	（动）	yùdào	encounter (a problem)
				出会う
				만나다.맞닥뜨리다
24.	平均	（形）	píngjūn	average
				平均
				평균
25.	以上		yǐshàng	and above, more than
				…以上
				이상
26.	提供	（动）	tígōng	to supply, to offer
				提供する
				제공하다.공급하다
27.	推荐信	（名）	tuījiànxìn	letter of recommendation
				推薦書
				추천서

28. 发表	（动）	fābiǎo	publish
			発表する
			글을 게재해다. 발표하다
29. 论文	（名）	lùnwén	thesis, academic paper
			論文
			논문
30. 成果	（名）	chéngguǒ	findings, results
			成果
			성과.결과
31. 志	（名）	zhì	aspiration, will
			志
			의지
32. 万	（数）	wàn	ten thousand
			万
			만
33. 原因	（名）	yuányīn	reason
			原因
			원인
34. 例如	（动）	lìrú	for example
			たとえば
			예를 들다
35. 导师	（名）	dǎoshī	adviser, professor
			勇気
			용기
36. 成才		chéng cái	become a success
			有用な人物になる
			인재가 되다. 쓸모 있는 사람이 되다

◆ 专有名词

1. 陈红		Chén Hóng	a name of Chinese
			陈红（人名）
			첸훙콩(인명)
2. 王丽		Wáng Lì	a name of Chinese
			王丽（人名）
			왕리(인명)

◆ 补充词语　Additional Words

1. 情况	（名）	qíngkuàng	situation
			ケース
			케이스

2. 毕业生	（名）	bìyèshēng	graduated student
			卒業生
			졸업생

3. 香山		Xiāng Shān	Fragrant Hill (the mountain's name)
			香山（北京郊外の山の名）
			향산

4. 长城		Chángchéng	Great Wall
			万里の長城
			만리장성

5. 清华大学		Qīnghuá Dàxué	Tsinghua University
			清華大学
			청화대학

6. 做人		zuò rén	being a man
			正しい人間になる
			사람이 되다

第十六课　为友谊干杯！

◆ 生 词　New Words

1. 友谊	（名）	yǒuyì	friendship
			友情、友好
			우정

2. 告别	（动）	gàobié	to say good-bye
			さよなら
			헤어지다

3. 久	（形）	jiǔ	long
			ロング
			긴

4. 丁	（名）	dīng	the 4th of the 10 heavenly Stems
			丁（順番をつけるときに用いる）
			정

5. 齐	（形）	qí	even, equal in length/height
			揃っている
			완전하게 되다, 완비되다

6. 首先	（副）	shǒuxiān	in the first
			最初に
			먼저

7. 预祝	（动）	yùzhù	in the first
			（…と）なるように祈る
			미리 축하하다

8. 早日	（副）	zǎorì	soon, at an early date 一日も早く 벌써
9. 流水	（名）	liúshuǐ	flowing water 流れる 흐르다
10. 一下子	（副）	yíxiàzi	all of sudden, all at once いっぺんに 한번에, 단번에
11. 学院	（名）	xuéyuàn	college 大学 단과 대학
12. 情景	（名）	qíngjǐng	scene, sight 情景、光景、ありさま 광경, 장면
13. 黄	（形）	huáng	yellow 黄色い 노란
14. 上衣	（名）	shàngyī	jacket 上着 윗 옷
15. 分(不清)	（动）	fēn	cannot recognize はっきり区別できない 분별할 수 없다
16. 句子	（名）	jùzi	sentence センテンス 문장
17. 笑话(儿)	（名）	xiàohua(r)	joke 笑い話、おかしなこと 농담
18. 流利	（形）	liúlì	fluentl 流暢である 유창하다
19. 舍不得		shěbude	to be loath to part with or give up 離れがない 아쉽다, 섭섭하다
20. 分别	（动）	fēnbié	to part, to leave each other 別れる 분별하다
21. 难过	（形）	nánguò	to feel sorry/bod/sad/grieved 苦しい、つらい 어렵다

22. 集合	（动）	jíhé	to get together 集合する 집합
23. 夫人	（名）	fūrén	Mrs., madam 夫人 부인
24. 问候	（动）	wènhòu	to say hello to 挨拶をする 안부하다
25. 交(朋友)	（动）	jiāo	make friends 友達になる 세계
26. 亲爱	（形）	qīn'ài	dear, beloved 親愛なる 친애하는, 사랑하는
27. 愿望	（名）	yuànwàng	wish 望み 희망, 원하고 바라다
28. 继续	（动）	jìxù	to continue 続く、継続する 계속하다
29. 情况	（名）	qíngkuàng	situation 状況、事情 상황

◆ 补充词语　Additional Words

1. 支	（量）	zhī	*measure word* 曲（歌や楽曲を数える量詞） 곡, 가지(본문중, 노래를 세는 단위)
2. 民歌	（名）	míngē	folk song 民間歌謡 민족의 노래
3. 杂志	（名）	zázhì	magazine 雑誌 잡지
4. 相聚	（动）	xiāngjù	to gather people together/gathering 互いに集う 모이다
5. 美好	（形）	měihǎo	beautiful, wonderful 美しい、素晴らしい 좋다.훌륭하다. 아름답다

6. 锁	（动）	suǒ	to lock
			鍵を閉める
			잠그다
7. 碰杯		pèng bēi	to clink glasses in a toast
			グラスを合わせる
			잔을 부딪히다
8. 闻	（动）	wén	to smell
			嗅ぐ
			냄새를 맡다
9. 香气	（名）	xiāngqì	fragrance
			香り
			향기

词语总表

词语 Words	词性 Part of speech	拼音 Phonetic Transcription	所在课 Lesson
A			
爱人	（名）	àirén	6
安静	（形）	ānjìng	2
安全	（形）	ānquán	3
按照	（介）	ànzhào	5
B			
白酒	（名）	báijiǔ	13
白头	（名）	báitóu	11
拜	（动）	bài	11
班长	（名）	bānzhǎng	5
傍晚	（名）	bàngwǎn	7
报名	（动）	bàomíng	5
报纸	（名）	bàozhǐ	10
北边	（名）	běibiān	3
备课		bèi kè	12
（几）比（几）	（动）	bǐ	2
比赛	（动）	bǐsài	2
笔	（名）	bǐ	10
必须	（副）	bìxū	15
毕业证	（名）	bìyèzhèng	10
变化	（动）	biànhuà	1
（手）表	（名）	biǎo	6
表现	（名）	biǎoxiàn	9
表扬	（动）	biǎoyáng	5
冰箱	（名）	bīngxiāng	13
丙	（名）	bǐng	4
并不	（副）	bìngbù	7
伯伯	（名）	bóbo	7
补充	（动）	bǔchōng	11
不但	（连）	búdàn	4
不好意思		bù hǎo yìsi	8
不久	（名）	bùjiǔ	4
不论……都……		búlùn……dōu……	4
不少		bù shǎo	10
不同	（形）	bùtóng	6

C

裁判	（名）	cáipàn	2
参观	（动）	cānguān	10
餐厅	（名）	cāntīng	4
叉	（名）	chā	13
差别	（名）	chābié	14
炒蘑菇		chǎo mógu	4
闯	（动）	chuǎng	3
成才		chéngcái	15
（足球）场	（名）	chǎng	2
成果	（名）	chéngguǒ	15
成绩	（名）	chéngjì	5
乘客	（名）	chéngkè	3
抽（烟）	（动）	chōu	9
出国		chū guó	15
出生	（动）	chūshēng	1
出事		chū shì	3
除了……以外	（连）	chúle……yǐwài	5
厨房	（名）	chúfáng	12
处理	（动）	chǔlǐ	9
词典	（名）	cídiǎn	15
从小	（副）	cóngxiǎo	4
存	（动）	cún	7
存在	（动）	cúnzài	9

D

打（基础）	（动）	dǎ	9
打（牌）	（动）	dǎ	12
大自然	（名）	dàzìrán	14
待	（动）	dāi	8
代沟	（名）	dàigōu	8
代替	（动）	dàitì	7
带（孩子）	（动）	dài	7
当	（动）	dāng	1
当地	（名）	dāngdì	15
刀	（名）	dāo	13
导师	（名）	dǎoshī	15
导游	（名）	dǎoyóu	12
到处	（名）	dàochù	9
到底	（副）	dàodǐ	14
电视剧	（名）	diànshìjù	12
……得很		……dehěn	4
钓（鱼）	（动）	diào	8

丁	（名）	dīng	16
动物	（名）	dòngwù	14
豆浆	（名）	dòujiāng	13
队	（名）	duì	2
队长	（名）	duìzhǎng	2
队员	（名）	duìyuán	2
对	（动）	duì	2
对面	（名）	duìmiàn	3

E

| 儿女 | （名） | érnǚ | 7 |

F

发表	（动）	fābiǎo	15
发声		fā shēng	5
发展	（动）	fāzhǎn	10
罚	（动）	fá	2
反	（形）	fǎn	3
反对	（动）	fǎnduì	7
饭店	（名）	fàndiàn	11
饭桌	（名）	fànzhuō	8
方法	（名）	fāngfǎ	5
方面	（名）	fāngmiàn	5
非……不可		fēi……bùkě	13
费	（动）	fèi	8
分（不清）	（动）	fēn	16
分别	（动）	fēnbié	16
……分之……		……fēnzhī……	11
份	（量）	fèn	6
丰富	（形）	fēngfù	4
风味	（名）	fēngwèi	13
夫人	（名）	fūrén	16
福	（名）	fú	1
负责	（动、形）	fùzé	10
附近	（名）	fùjìn	8
复印	（动）	fùyìn	6
复杂	（形）	fùzá	9

G

改变	（动）	gǎibiàn	9
干杯		gān bēi	11
感到	（动）	gǎndào	1
感动	（动）	gǎndòng	7
感觉	（动）	gǎnjué	13

感情	(名)	gǎnqíng	14
告别	(动)	gàobié	16
歌迷	(名)	gēmí	12
歌曲	(名)	gēqǔ	12
歌手	(名)	gēshǒu	5
各(种)	(代)	gè(zhǒng)	8
工业	(名)	gōngyè	14
工作日	(名)	gōngzuòrì	15
狗	(名)	gǒu	14
古迹	(名)	gǔjì	12
故事	(名)	gùshì	11
怪不得		guàibude	11
关照	(动)	guānzhào	1
管	(动)	guǎn	6
(看不)惯	(形)	guàn	8
(掉)光	(形)	guāng	7
广泛	(形)	guǎngfàn	11
规则	(名)	guīzé	3
贵(公司)	(形)	guì	10
国界	(名)	guójiè	6
果汁	(名)	guǒzhī	13
过去	(名)	guòqù	8

H

喊	(动)	hǎn	2
好处	(名)	hǎochù	13
好多	(数)	hǎoduō	7
好听	(形)	hǎotīng	1
合唱	(名)	héchàng	5
和美	(形)	héměi	11
红灯	(名)	hóngdēng	3
红红绿绿		hónghóng lǜlǜ	7
后	(名)	hòu	3
护照	(名)	hùzhào	15
华裔	(名)	huáyì	1
话题	(名)	huàtí	9
环境	(名)	huánjìng	14
黄	(形)	huáng	16
黄牌儿	(名)	huángpáir	2
回复	(动)	huífù	15
婚礼	(名)	hūnlǐ	11
婚姻	(名)	hūnyīn	11
活	(形)	huó	15
活动	(动、名)	huódòng	5

(干)活儿	(名)	huór	9

J

鸡	(名)	jī	13
集	(量)	jí	12
集合	(动)	jíhé	16
挤	(动)	jǐ	14
技术	(名)	jìshù	10
既……也……	(连)	jì……yě……	9
继续	(动)	jìxù	16
家务	(名)	jiāwù	9
家乡	(名)	jiāxiāng	1
甲	(名)	jiǎ	4
假期	(名)	jiàqī	1
嫁	(动)	jià	9
尖椒牛肉		jiānjiāo niúròu	4
坚持	(动)	jiānchí	13
间	(量)	jiān	14
减肥		jiǎn féi	13
简历	(名)	jiǎnlì	10
(复印)件	(名)	jiàn	10
健身	(动)	jiànshēn	12
建议	(动)	jiànyì	13
奖学金	(名)	jiǎngxuéjīn	15
交(朋友)	(动)	jiāo	16
叫	(动)	jiào	2
教师	(名)	jiàoshī	12
教育	(动、名)	jiàoyù	6
接着	(动)	jiēzhe	1
节日	(名)	jiérì	4
结果	(连)	jiéguǒ	3
结束	(动)	jiéshù	2
今后	(名)	jīnhòu	9
金	(名)	jīn	1
进(球)	(名)	jìn	2
进行	(动)	jìnxíng	2
经过	(名、动)	jīngguò	11
经济	(名)	jīngjì	9
经理	(名)	jīnglǐ	10
经历	(名)	jīnglì	8
精彩	(形)	jīngcǎi	11
静	(形)	jìng	12
久	(形)	jiǔ	16
酒	(名)	jiǔ	3

举（杯）	（动）	jǔ	11
举行	（动）	jǔxíng	4
句子	（名）	jùzi	16
聚	（动）	jù	1
聚会	（动、名）	jùhuì	1
捐	（动）	juān	7
决定	（名）	juédìng	14

K

开（车）	（动）	kāi	3
开心	（形）	kāixīn	1
考虑	（动）	kǎolǜ	7
科学	（名、形）	kēxué	12
可乐	（名）	kělè	4
可怕	（形）	kěpà	7
渴	（形）	kě	4
客人	（名）	kèrén	10
客厅	（名）	kètīng	14
课外	（名）	kèwài	5
口福	（名）	kǒufú	13
苦	（形）	kǔ	14
夸	（动）	kuā	6
筷子	（名）	kuàizi	13

L

拉拉队	（名）	lālāduì	2
篮球	（名）	lánqiú	12
浪漫	（形）	làngmàn	11
劳动	（动）	láodòng	14
劳驾		láo jià	3
老	（形）	lǎo	7
老板	（名）	lǎobǎn	4
老年	（名）	lǎonián	8
（一周）来	（助）	lái	8
……来说		……láishuō	12
理解	（动）	lǐjiě	7
理由	（名）	lǐyóu	6
利用	（动）	lìyòng	8
例如	（动）	lìrú	15
连……也……		lián……yě……	9
练（书法）	（动）	liàn	7
恋爱	（动）	liàn'ài	11
恋人	（名）	liàn rén	11
邻居	（名）	línjū	2

领导	（名）	lǐngdǎo	10
另	（形）	lìng	6
另外	（形）	lìngwài	1
流利	（形）	liúlì	16
流水	（动）	liúshuǐ	16
龙（船）	（名）	lóng	4
录取	（动）	lùqǔ	15
路	（量）	lù	14
路过	（动）	lùguò	4
旅游	（动）	lǚyóu	7
律师	（名）	lǜshī	12
论文	（名）	lùnwén	15
落后	（形）	luòhòu	5

M

麻将	（名）	májiàng	12
马	（名）	mǎ	14
满分	（名）	mǎnfēn	6
猫	（名）	māo	14
梦想	（名）	mèngxiǎng	5
迷	（动）	mí	12
秘书	（名）	mìshū	10
面包	（名）	miànbāo	13
面试	（动）	miànshì	10
面谈	（动）	miàntán	15
面条儿	（名）	miàntiáor	13
民族	（名）	mínzú	4
名	（量）	míng	5
名胜	（名）	míngshèng	12
明白	（动、形）	míngbai	6
模范	（名）	mófàn	9
蘑菇	（名）	mógu	4
目前	（名）	mùqián	9

N

那里	（代）	nàlǐ	14
奶奶	（名）	nǎinai	4
男人	（名）	nánrén	9
南边	（名）	nánbiān	3
难道	（副）	nándào	12
难过	（形）	nánguò	16
能力	（名）	nénglì	10
年龄	（名）	niánlíng	10
牛奶	（名）	niúnǎi	13

农村	（名）	nóngcūn	14
农民	（名）	nóngmín	14
农业	（名）	nóngyè	14
女人	（名）	nǚrén	9

P

排队		pái duì	4
排球	（名）	páiqiú	12
牌	（名）	pái	12
牌子	（名）	páizi	4
培养	（动）	péiyǎng	8
碰见		pèng jiàn	1
批评	（动）	pīpíng	9
撇	（名）	piě	15
平安	（形）	píng'ān	3
平等	（形）	píngděng	9
平均	（形）	píngjūn	15
葡萄酒	（名）	pǔtaojiǔ	13
普通话	（名）	pǔtōnghuà	1

Q

齐	（形）	qí	16
其他	（代）	qítā	12
其中	（代）	qízhōng	10
奇怪	（形）	qíguài	12
气	（动）	qì	9
起	（量）	qǐ	3
千万	（副）	qiānwàn	8
签证	（名）	qiānzhèng	15
前途	（名）	qiántú	10
强	（形）	qiáng	13
敲	（动）	qiāo	2
切	（动）	qiē	13
亲爱	（形）	qīn'ài	16
亲切	（形）	qīnqiè	1
轻伤	（名）	qīngshāng	3
情景	（名）	qíngjǐng	16
情况	（名）	qíngkuàng	16
穷	（形）	qióng	7
全额	（名）	quán'é	15
劝（架）	（名）	quàn	9
却	（副）	què	14
确实	（副）	quèshí	6

R

热闹	（形）	rènao	1
人家	（代）	rénjia	7
认错		rèn cuò	9
认为	（动）	rènwéi	9
日子	（名）	rìzi	11

S

沙发	（名）	shāfā	9
晒	（动）	shài	12
伤	（动、名）	shāng	3
商场	（名）	shāngchǎng	8
商量	（动）	shāngliang	7
上（百）	（动）	shàng	11
上班		shàng bān	3
上面	（名）	shàngmiàn	4
上衣	（名）	shàngyī	16
舍不得		shěbude	16
社会	（名）	shèhuì	9
申请	（动）	shēnqǐng	15
申请书	（名）	shēnqǐngshū	15
身材	（名）	shēncái	13
生产	（动）	shēngchǎn	14
声音	（名）	shēngyīn	5
剩（下）	（动）	shèng	7
十分	（副）	shífēn	4
实践	（动、名）	shíjiàn	12
实现	（动）	shíxiàn	5
市	（名）	shì	3
……似的	（助）	……shìde	14
事故	（名）	shìgù	3
收获	（名）	shōuhuò	8
收入	（名）	shōurù	10
收拾	（动）	shōushi	8
首先	（副）	shǒuxiān	16
受（教育）	（动）	shòu	6
售票员	（名）	shòupiàoyuán	3
书本	（名）	shūběn	8
书房	（名）	shūfáng	12
输	（动）	shū	2
熟悉	（动）	shúxī	10
数学	（名）	shùxué	5
摔	（动）	shuāi	2
顺	（形）	shùn	11

说明	（动）	shuōmíng	11
硕士	（名）	shòushì	15
速度	（名）	sùdù	6

T

讨论	（动）	tǎolùn	9
套	（量）	tào	14
特产	（名）	tèchǎn	1
特点	（名）	tèdiǎn	9
踢	（动）	tī	2
提供	（动）	tígōng	15
题目	（名）	tímù	9
天生	（形）	tiānshēng	11
跳舞		tiào wǔ	7
通知	（动）	tōngzhī	10
通知书	（名）	tōngzhīshū	15
同班		tóng bān	11
同事	（名）	tóngshì	8
痛快	（形）	tòngkuai	8
突然	（形）	tūrán	11
团聚	（动）	tuánjù	8
推	（动）	tuī	2
推荐信	（名）	tuījiànxìn	15
退休	（动）	tuìxiū	12

W

外卖	（名）	wàimài	4
外语	（名）	wàiyǔ	5
万	（数）	wàn	15
危险	（形）	wēixiǎn	3
卫生间	（名）	wèishēngjiān	14
喂	（动）	wèi	14
文化	（名）	wénhuà	6
问好		wèn hǎo	1
问候	（动）	wènhòu	16
握手		wò shǒu	2

X

西餐	（名）	xīcān	13
洗（衣服）	（动）	xǐ	8
洗衣机	（名）	xǐyījī	8
喜酒	（名）	xǐjiǔ	11
喜事	（名）	xǐshì	11

喜糖	（名）	xǐtáng	11
下班		xià bān	6
下边	（名）	xiàbian	1
下载	（动）	xiàzài	12
现代	（名）	xiàndài	9
现象	（名）	xiànxiàng	9
羡慕	（形）	xiànmù	7
相爱	（动）	xiāng'ài	6
相同	（形）	xiāngtóng	12
想法	（名）	xiǎngfǎ	6
想念	（动）	xiǎngniàn	4
向	（介）	xiàng	1
消息	（名）	xiāoxi	5
小时候	（名）	xiǎo shíhou	1
小学	（名）	xiǎoxué	14
校园	（名）	xiàoyuán	2
笑话	（动）	xiàohua	13
笑话（儿）	（名）	xiàohua(r)	16
心	（名）	xīn	6
心事	（名）	xīnshì	6
辛苦	（形）	xīnkǔ	1
新郎	（名）	xīnláng	11
新娘	（名）	xīnniáng	11
新人	（名）	xīnrén	11
新闻	（名）	xīnwén	3
新鲜	（形）	xīnxiān	14
行	（动）	xíng	11
行李	（名）	xíngli	1
兴趣	（名）	xìngqù	5
幸福	（形）	xìngfú	1
性格	（名）	xìnggé	6
选	（动）	xuǎn	5
选择	（动）	xuǎnzé	6
学院	（名）	xuéyuàn	16

Y

严重	（形）	yánzhòng	14
演讲	（动）	yǎnjiǎng	9
宴会	（名）	yànhuì	11
羊	（名）	yáng	14
阳台	（名）	yángtái	12
养	（动）	yǎng	14
养老院	（名）	yǎnglǎoyuàn	7
要不	（连）	yàobù	8

要求	（动）	yāoqiú	15
爷爷	（名）	yéye	1
也许	（副）	yěxǔ	4
一下子	（副）	yíxiàzi	16
乙	（名）	yǐ	4
以上		yǐshàng	15
意见	（名）	yìjiàn	14
意义	（名）	yìyì	11
银	（名）	yín	1
银行	（名）	yínháng	7
饮食	（名）	yǐnshí	13
印象	（名）	yìnxiàng	10
营养	（名）	yíngyǎng	4
赢	（动）	yíng	2
影响	（动）	yǐngxiǎng	2
拥抱	（动）	yōngbào	2
优美	（形）	yōuměi	14
由（……组成）	（介）	yóu	2
邮件	（名）	yóujiàn	15
油条	（名）	yóutiáo	13
游览	（动）	yóulǎn	12
友谊	（名）	yǒuyì	16
有的是		yǒudeshì	6
有些	（代）	yǒuxiē	6
有意思		yǒu yìsi	1
有用		yǒu yòng	7
右手	（名）	yòushǒu	13
语文	（名）	yǔwén	5
语言	（名）	yǔyán	15
预祝	（动）	yùzhù	16
遇到	（动）	yùdào	15
原谅	（动）	yuánliàng	6
原因	（名）	yuányīn	15
愿望	（名）	yuànwàng	16
愿意	（动）	yuànyì	6
约会	（名）	yuēhuì	6

Z

再婚	（动）	zàihūn	7
早日	（副）	zǎorì	16
怎样	（代）	zěnyàng	7
增加	（动）	zēngjiā	10
展览	（名）	zhǎnlǎn	8
占	（动）	zhàn	11
站	（动）	zhàn	2

(车)站	(名)	(chē)zhàn	3
招	(动)	zhāo	10
照顾	(动)	zhàogù	7
这些	(代)	zhèxiē	7
真心	(名)	zhēnxīn	6
真正	(形)	zhēnzhèng	9
正(因为)	(副)	zhèng	6
证明	(名)	zhèngmíng	10
证明	(动)	zhèngmíng	12
政治	(名)	zhèngzhì	9
之间	(名)	zhījiān	8
支持	(动)	zhīchí	2
职员	(名)	zhíyuán	10
只好	(副)	zhǐhǎo	8
只有	(连)	zhǐyǒu	13
纸	(名)	zhǐ	10
志	(名)	zhì	15
中餐	(名)	zhōngcān	13
中年	(名)	zhōngnián	10
中心	(名)	zhōngxīn	12
重伤	(名)	zhòngshāng	3
重视	(动)	zhòngshì	11
周围	(名)	zhōuwéi	6
周五	(名)	zhōuwǔ	8
周一	(名)	zhōuyī	8
主持	(动)	zhǔchí	11
主婚人	(名)	zhǔhūnrén	11
主人	(名)	zhǔrén	13
主食	(名)	zhǔshí	4
主要	(形)	zhǔyào	12
准	(动)	zhǔn	3
自杀	(动)	zìshā	7
自由	(名、形)	zìyóu	7
自助餐	(名)	zìzhùcān	13
总(是)	(副)	zǒng	6
粽子	(名)	zòngzi	4
租	(动)	zū	15
足球	(名)	zúqiú	2
组	(名)	zǔ	5
组成	(动)	zǔchéng	2
醉	(动)	zuì	13
尊重	(动)	zūnzhòng	6
遵守	(动)	zūnshǒu	3
左手	(名)	zuǒshǒu	13
做客		zuò kè	13

量　词　表

量词 Nouns	拼音 Phonetic Transcription	对应的名词 Measure words
1. 把	bǎ	叉子、刀
2. 包	bāo	糖、喜糖、烟
3. 杯	bēi	白酒、豆浆、果汁、矿泉水、牛奶、啤酒、葡萄酒、喜酒
4. 本	běn	护照、词典
5. 笔	bǐ	奖学金、收入
6. 部	bù	词典、电视剧
7. 场	chǎng	比赛、聚会、恋爱、球赛
8. 次	cì	比赛、婚礼、婚姻、活动、恋爱、面试、球赛、事故、演讲、宴会、约会
9. 处	chù	古迹、名胜
10. 袋	dài	豆浆、面包、牛奶、喜糖
11. 点儿	diǎnr	差别、成绩、代沟、改变、感情、果汁、好处、活儿、家务、基础、技术、理由、困难、面包、牛奶、能力、葡萄酒、收获、想法、消息、心事、印象、影响、原因、自由
12. 段	duàn	国界、婚姻、假期、经过、经历、历史、路、日子、友谊
13. 堆	duī	书本、行李
14. 对	duì	恋人、沙发、新人
15. 顿	dùn	西餐、喜酒、中餐、自助餐
16. 份	fèn	报、报纸、毕业证、复印件、感情、简历、奖学金、快递、牛肉、牛奶、申请书、收入、通知、通知书、外卖、西餐、喜糖、演讲稿、邮件、友谊、证明、中餐、主食
17. 封	fēng	推荐信、邮件
18. 副	fù	麻将、牌
19. 个	gè	班长、傍晚、毕业证、冰箱、博士、裁判、叉子、餐厅、成果、乘客、传统、厨房、大自然、电视剧、队、队长、队员、导师、导游、动物、饭桌、方法、方面、歌迷、工作日、好处、华裔、话题、环境、黄牌儿、婚礼、活动、基础、机场、家乡、假期、建议、教师、节日、结果、经理、聚会、句子、决定、客人、客厅、困难、拉拉队、篮球、老板、老人、老先生、理想、理由、恋人、邻居、领导、梦想、模范、秘书、面包、民族、奶奶、男人、农村、农民、女人、排球、牌子、签证、前途、青年、情景、情况、沙发、商场、社会、市、事故、收获、售票员、说明、书房、硕士、特点、题目、通知、同事、卫生间、洗衣机、现象、想法、消息、笑话、校园、新郎、新娘、新人、心事、行李、学院、宴会、阳台、养老院、爷爷、要求、意义、印象、邮件、原因、愿望、约会、早上、展览、证明、职员、中心、主婚人、主人、粽子、足球、足球场
20. 根	gēn	油条

21. 盒	hé	笔、牛奶、喜糖、烟
22. 户	hù	邻居
23. 级	jí	裁判、教师
24. 集	jí	电视剧
25. 家	jiā	茶馆、餐厅、饭店、邻居、商场、银行
26. 架	jià	飞机
27. 间	jiān	厨房、客厅、卫生间
28. 件	jiàn	家务、快递、事故、喜事、新闻、行李、证明
29. 斤	jīn	白酒、面条儿、蘑菇、牛肉、喜糖、粽子
30. 颗	kē	心、真心
31. 克	kè	黄金、面包、面条儿、牛肉、喜糖、白银
32. 口	kǒu	白酒、刀、豆浆、矿泉水、果汁、面包、面条儿、牛奶、牛肉、啤酒、葡萄酒、喜酒
33. 块	kuài	面包、牛肉、手表、喜糖
34. 两	liǎng	白酒、金、面条儿、蘑菇、牛肉
35. 门	mén	技术、科学、课、外语、学术、艺术、语言
36. 名	míng	博士、裁判、乘客、导师、导演、导游、律师、青年、售票员、硕士、职员
37. 盘	pán	牛肉、主食
38. 匹	pǐ	马
39. 篇	piān	论文、演讲稿
40. 片	piàn	面包、牛肉、真心
41. 瓶	píng	白酒、果汁、矿泉水、牛奶、啤酒、葡萄酒
42. 起	qǐ	事故
43. 群	qún	动物、狗、猫、牛、羊
44. 首	shǒu	歌曲
45. 双	shuāng	儿女、筷子
46. 所	suǒ	小学、校园、学院、养老院
47. 台	tái	洗衣机
48. 套	tào	沙发
49. 条	tiáo	狗、国界、建议、理由、龙、龙船、路、消息、新闻、烟、意见
50. 碗	wǎn	豆浆、面条儿、牛奶
51. 位	wèi	班长、伯伯、裁判、乘客、导师、导游、队长、队员、夫人、歌迷、教师、经理、客人、老板、老人、老先生、领导、律师、模范、秘书、奶奶、青年、农民、同事、新郎、新娘、新人、爷爷、主婚人、主人
52. 箱	xiāng	白酒、矿泉水、啤酒
53. 些	xiē	变化、差别、成绩、乘客、代沟、改变、活儿、基础、奖学金、教育、经历、口福、困难、理由、能力、日子、收获、收入、售票员、书本、说明、特产、文化、想法、消息、心事、行李、印象、影响、营养、原因、知识、自由
54. 盏	zhǎn	红灯
55. 张	zhāng	毕业证、报、报纸、表格、复印件、合影、黄牌儿、机票、通知

书、纸

56. 支	zhī	笔、歌曲、拉拉队、烟、右手、足球队、左手
57. 只	zhī	狗、鸡、龙船、猫、手表、羊、右手、左手
58. 种	zhǒng	笔、表现、词典、动物、方法、风味、感觉、感情、工业、关系、果汁、好处、环境、活动、技术、家务、奖学金、教育、经济、经历、科学、困难、梦想、蘑菇、能力、前途、情景、情况、葡萄酒、社会、身材、手表、特产、外语、危险、文化、现象、想法、新闻、性格、学术、烟、艺术、意义、饮食、印象、营养、友谊、语言、原因、愿望、政治、知识、自由、主食
59. 桌	zhuō	麻将、西餐、喜酒、中餐
60. 座	zuò	古迹、机场、名胜、商场

Lesson one   I Had a Good Winter Vacation

(The first day, just before class)

Teacher:	We have some new students. Welcome! Why don't you all get to know each other?
Peter:	We've already met.
Teacher:	Oh? Then introduce them to me, please.
Peter:	This student is Korean. His name is Kim... Kim something or other. I'm sorry; your name is a little hard to remember.
Kim Yunfu:	Kim Yunfu. "Jin" as in "jinyin" (gold and silver), "Yun" as in "baiyun"(white cloud), "fu" as in "xingfu"(fortune).
Peter:	Yes, yes, Kim Yunfu. (Pointing to another student) She is...
Yamada yumi:	My name is Yamada yumi. I'm Japanese.
Teacher:	Both of you have good names. Who is the next one?
Wu Pingchun:	It's my turn. I'm a Chinese American. I can speak a little Cantonese, but I want to learn Mandarin.
Peter:	And your name?
Wu Pingchun:	Wu Pingchun. "Wu", (the structure of Chinese character) are the "mouth"and "heaven". "Ping"as in"shuiping" (level) and "chun" as in "Chuntian" (spring).
Kim Yunfu:	(whispering to Peter) How is this class?
Peter:	Don't worry, our class is very friendly, and the teacher is like a friend to us, too.

(In the dorm)

Lisa:	I'm back, Annie!
Annie:	Wow, put your baggage down, please. I thought you had get back earlier than I. How was it? I bet you had a really good time, didn't you?
Lisa:	Certainly! It was really interesting.
Annie:	Let me look at you. Oh, you're thinner than before, and darker, but even perkier!
Lisa:	Let's not only talk about me. How was your winter vacation? Is your family all right?
Annie:	They're all fine, thank you. Oh, this is something my parents asked me to bring for you. It's a local product from my hometown. They also say hello to you.
Lisa:	Your parents are so nice! To be honest, I really miss my parents when I was travelling along. Ok, when is summer vacation?
Annie:	Look at you, we haven't even started school yet and you're already thinking of another vacation. I saw Jeff yesterday and he said we had better get together after you came back.

(At a party)

Peter:	I haven't seen you for a long time, Jeff. Did you go home over the vacation or did you go travelling?
Jeff:	Neither. I didn't go anywhere.
Peter:	Such a long break, and you didn't go anywhere?
Jeff:	You'll never guess what I did. I became a teacher and taught English.
Peter:	You? A teacher?
Jeff:	You don't believe me, do you? But the students really like me.
Peter:	What did you think of being a teacher?
Jeff:	The job is tough and enjoyable.
Jin Yunfu:	Peter, which one is Wang Ping? You always said he is an interesting man, could you please introduce him to me?
Peter:	Oh my, I forgot all about that. Ok, let me introduce you to him.

I had a really good time this winter vacation. Spring festival was my grandfather's 80th birthday. All of my family returned to our hometown where there are more lively activities celebrating Spring Festival than those in Beijing. I felt particularly warm when I went back where I was born and I lived throughout my childhood. My hometown has changed a lot. My childhood friends have all grown up, I had a hard time recognizing them.

Lesson Two   It's Not Certain yet Who'll Win!

(At home)

Husband: Good shot! Come on!

Wife: Listen, it sounds like someone's knocking at the door.

Husband: Ok, go to see who is it.

Neighbor: Sorry, could you turn off your TV? My mother is ill and needs to have a rest...

Wife: Oh, We are really sorry for bothering your mother.

Husband: I'm truly sorry; I just can't keep from cheering when I watch a game...

Neighbor: I'm also a sports fan, just like you. Uh, what's the score?

(On the campus)

Peter: Come on, let's go to watch a game.

Jin Yunfu: Where is it?

Peter: It's at the football field.

Jin Yunfu: Who vs. who?

Peter: The international team against the school varsity team.

Jin Yunfu: The international team?

Peter: Yeah, it's a team of foreign students. They play very well.

Jin Yunfu: Can they defeat the school varsity?

Peter: The international team is quite good too. But it's not certain who'll win.

(At the football field)

Jin Yunfu: The game begins.

Peter: International team, COME ON!

Jin Ynufu: Aw, number 7 tripped! Quick, get up!

Peter: He's Ok, see how easily he got up.

Jin Yunfu: Ah, how could number 13 have pushed that player?

Peter: The referee is giving him a yellow card to punish him.

Jin Yunfu: That's fair.

Peter: Good! They scored!

(The captain says)

I'm the captain of the international soccer team. Every member in my team is great. Generally we have a game once every two weeks and everyone plays seriously. My girl friend is a head of the cheerleaders. We have more energy during the competition with their enthusiastic help. Just like today, at the beginning, everyone was very nervous, afraid of losing the game. At this time, I heard the cheerleader team cheering us on. I thought: "The international team will definitely win". As the game was about to end, our team once again kicked a ball into the goal. Two to one, our team won! Everybody was shaking hands and hugging each other. We were terrible happy then!

Lesson Three   Could You Please Pull Over for Me?

(On the bus)

Passenger: Excuse me, Sir. Does this bus go to the zoo?

Conductor: You're in the wrong direction. The zoo is in the south but we are going to the north. You can get off this one and catch a bus on the other side of the street.

Passenger: Oh, May I trouble you to stop the bus here, please?

Conductor: No, the bus is not allowed to stop anywhere except bus stations.

Passenger: I took the wrong bus, quick, let me off!

Conductor: I'm sorry about that, but I don't mean to be helpless to you. On the road I can't stop the bus.

(A taxi driver returns home late)

Wife: How come you came back home so late?

Husband: It was a really unfortunate day today. I got fined.

Wife: What? What happened?

Husband: Accidentally ran a red light.

Wife: You didn't hurt anyone, did you?

Husband: No!

Wife: In the future be more careful. You have to always remember: " Go to work happily, return home safely". It would let us not worry about you everyday.

Husband: OK, from now on I'll pay attention to and follow traffic rules, so you don't worry.

(Traffic News broadcasting)

This afternoon, another traffic accident occurred in our city. A driver of a car was drunk driving when he ran a red light and crashed into a bus travelling from south to north. One person was serious injured, and two people were injured. We urge drivers to observe traffic safety. Please don't drive after drinking and don't run red lights, for it is too dangerous.

Lesson Four   I Didn't Like Eating Fish Since I Was Little

(In the cafeteria)

A: Come on, what are we going to eat? The waitress is waiting.

B: I'll have stir-fried beef with pepper, OK?

A: Good. I like eating spicy things. I'd like to get some stir-fried mushrooms.

C: And have a fish, please.

A: I didn't like eating fish since I was little. No matter how it is made, I just don't like eating it.

C: The fish here is good, try it once, you might become like it.

B: Have one fish then. Fish are nutritious. Everybody says fish is good to brain. It makes people smarter.

A: Is there still time to feed my brain? Ok, I'll eat with you. If you want to get one, then do it.

C: Three dishes are enough. And have three cups of Coca-Cola. What do you want for staple food?

A: A bowl of rice for each of us.

B: I'm starving and thirsty now. Waitress, would you hurry up, please?

(Jeff and Wang Ping are chatting)

Jeff: China has a long history and many minorities, are there many traditional festivals and many minority holidays too?

Wang Ping: Yes, tomorrow is a holiday.

Jeff: Really? What is it?

Wang Ping: Duanwu Festival, it's the "Dragon boat Festival" in English.

Jeff: Do we get a day off?

Wang Ping:	Yes, it is interesting as everyone eats "zongzi". There are some areas holding boating competitions.
Jeff:	What is "zongzi"?
Wang Ping:	"Zongzi", um... Ok, my grandmother makes it every year. I'll invite you to my home tomorrow; we'll make and eat "zongzi" together.

(At Wang Ping's home)

Grandmother:	The "zongzi" are finished. All of you can taste them now.
Jeff:	I have never eaten it before. It's so delicious.
Wang Ping:	Don't eat too much even though it's delicious. There are many dishes waiting for you.
Jeff:	All of us were making "zongzi" just now. Who cooked so many dishes?
Wang Ping:	I ordered take out.
Jeff:	order take out? That is good idea!
Wang Ping:	If you don't have time to line up at dinning hall some day, you can make a phone call to order take out. It's very fast and convenient.
Grandmother:	Come on, Wang Ping. Don't talk anymore. Let your guests eat more now.

(Jeff says)

There is a small restaurant outside school. It's hasn't been opened too long. One day when I was walking around, in front of the restaurant, I found a sign on the door. What was written on it was really interesting: "If you're satisfied with eating here, please tell your friends; if you're not satisfied with what you're eating here, please tell the manager." Then I went in and ordered one dish and one soup. They tasted pretty good and the price was quite cheap too. The service there is better than other restaurants as well. I went there many times afterwards, and satisfied every time. The boss of the restaurant already knows what I like to eat. He also said that after I go back home country I would definitely miss his restaurant.

Lesson Five   How Happy You Are

(At home)

Boy:	Mom, mom, I have a good news!
Mother:	Look, how happy you are! What's the good news?
Boy:	I had my test scores today. I got a 98 in language, 100 in math and 96 in foreign language. I am ranked first in the class and the teacher commended me as well.
Mother:	Good boy, congratulations. Mom will make some favorite dishes for you now.
Boy:	Can I help?
Mother:	No, no need. You can play for a while. Your dad will be back in minutes, it'll make him happy too.
Boy:	OK, then I'm going to play on the computer.

(Father comes back home)

Father:	How come there're many good things to eat?
Boy:	Something good. Guess, dad.
Father:	Hmm, you got me. (I can't guess it.)
Mother:	Let me tell you, our son is ranked first in the class this time. I think he has definitely become an advanced student.
Father:	Good boy! Tell me, what did you get?
Boy:	98 in language, 100 in math and 96 in foreign language.
Father:	You tested pretty well, but you still need to continue working hard!
Boy:	I know. Dad, Mom even cheered me on!
Dad:	Son, aside from studying hard you can't fall behind in other matters either.
Boy:	Of course, I'm our school's soccer team captain, as well as a chorus member. This semester I also was selected as our class captain.
Father and mother:	Good, good, let's go son!

(The child says to his father)

Our school has many extra-curricular clubs, every club has a teacher acting as a counselor. Students can sign up and participate according to their interests. Today, I signed up to participate in the chorus club, it was my first time participating in a chorus club activity the counselor said I have a great voice, but my singing method was not right. The teacher taught us a vocal articulation method, I tried it and found a great improvement. Starting today, I am going to practice hard, and in the future I will be the best singer and make my dream come true.

Lesson Six   Sorry, I'm Late

(At the gate of a movie theater)

Young Guy: I'm sorry I'm late. Are you upset?

Young Girl: Why do you always come late? Look at your watch. What time is it?

Young Guy: I'm really sorry, just when I was about to get off work, the manager wanted me to copy some things. I copied them as fast as I could. And when I came out, I discovered that there was no air in my bike; so I took a taxi, and ran into a traffic jam. Don't you think that's terrible?

Young Girl: Oh! You've always got so many excuses.

Young Guy: OK, don't be angry, forgive me, next time...

Young Girl: You are late all the time, no one will believe you next time. Do you think I have enough time to wait around for you?

Young Guy: Hey, don't move! Quick, take out your mirror!

Young Girl: What are you doing?

Young Guy: Look at your angry face. How pretty it is!

Young Girl: (laugh) Your...

(In the female students' dorm)

A: Why aren't you asleep yet?

B: I can't sleep. Will you talk with me?

A: Sure. I guess you've got something on your mind.

B: Oh, I sent my mom an e-mail and told her I have a boyfriend. After I sent the e-mail, I was a little worried.

A: Of course she'll be happy for you, what are you worrying about?

B: I know that. But I'm worried about something else.

A: What?

B: We're not from the same country; we have different culture background and habits. My mom will definitely disagree with my choice.

A: Haven't you heard "love knows no boundaries"? What's important is that you really love each other. Even though your cultures and custom are different, aren't you two happy together? That's all I'm saying. What does it matter what others think?

B: But my mom isn't one of those "others"?

A: It is because she's a mom that she has great hopes for your happiness and good fortune. You have to think of a way to let her understand that he is your ideal man and you two were meant for each other, and the needlessly worrying doesn't solve any problems.

B: You're right. I'm definitely bringing him home to meet my mom this summer. I believe he'll be accepted.

(B is talking with her mother on the phone)

Mom, I received your letter. I thought early on that you wouldn't agree. Please listen to what I think. Even though he is a foreigner, he's willing to respect our custom, and he's already decided not to eat pork. Of course he is a foreigner, but he is willing to respect our people's traditions. And also he's very well educated, he's a good person, has a good heart and personality, and his friends are not bad either. I'm not exaggerating about him, when the time comes and I bring him home to meet you, you'll be able to trust me and see that he is indeed worth to win my love.

Lesson Seven Health and Happiness Are More Important Than Anything

(Two people are chatting. A is a foreigner and B is a Chinese.)

A: I've discovered that old Chinese people really like to dance.

B: How did you find that out?

A: Every day, no matter if it's morning or evening, you can always see old people in colorful clothing dancing in the parks. Very interesting.

B: It's not all of the old people like to dance. Many active old people like climbing or walking or something else.

A: What do the inactive old people do?

B: Some of them like painting or doing calligraphy. Some of them take care of their grandchildren as a help to their son or daughter.

A: The way I see it, the issue isn't active or inactive. The most important is that the mind doesn't get old! Being old in mind is scarier than other things.

B: Right. I often see older foreigners coming to China to travel, they are quite old, their hair is all white, but they are in such good spirit, it's very admirable.

A: Of course these kinds of people are fortunate, but there aren't so many old people who can go out.

B: Then how do old people in general get along with? Do some people go to the nursing home?

A: Yes. But some of them don't want to go. They think that there is no place as good as home.

(At home)

Son: Mom, why are you crying?

Mom: Oh, it's nothing. It was just something I was watching on TV.

Son: What show moved you so much?

Mom: The TV show was talking about an old lady. Her husband was dead for many years. She worked hard to raise her children. There was an old man who was nice to her, and who thought about starting a new life with her, but the kids all opposed. She couldn't take it, and she committed suicide.

Son: Why didn't their kids think more about what is good for their parents? How couldn't they hope for their parents' good fortune?

Mom: Yes, there aren't many young people who really understand old people.

Son: Speaking of that, there's something I wanted to discuss with you.

Mom: What is it? And why do you look so serious?

Son: I think Uncle Liu is so good to you, always concerns and takes care of you. He also has those feelings, why don't you think about it?

Mom: Uh... oh, I know what he means, but...

Son: What are you worried about?

Mom: I'm worried that you'll have something to say about it. And what's more, it's enough that I have you.

Son: But a son's love can't replace a husband's love.

Mom: And also, how do the others see it?

Son: Older people also have the right to remarriage. Don't be afraid of this and that. What's most important is that you feel blessed, don't care about others' opinion. I sincerely hope you lead a happy life!

(A happy aged person says)

People ask me often why I don't deposit money in the bank? What am I thinking? My health is pretty good right now, no serious illnesses, why not eat better and go out to see more exciting places? Otherwise, if I wait till I'm older, when I can't move, and my teeth are all gone, and I have to use this money to get shots and take medicine and stay in hospitals... that's no exciting, is it? Except for eating and having a good time, The remaining money I will just donate. I think, I have no children, and if I save this money, I can't take it with me when I pass away, so it would be better helping those poor kids go to school. Using money in useful places really makes me feel very happy. People don't realize till they're old that health and happiness are more important than anything.

Lesson Eight   How to Spend the Weekend?

(Friday, two colleagues on the way back home after getting off work)

A: What did you do this weekend?

B: Went home to see my parents.

A: You seem to go back home every weekend.

B: Yeah, when family together there's a lot of happiness on. Such as cooking, watching TV, straightening up the louse, and chatting at the dinner table.

A: Wouldn't you like to relax by yourself?

B: I've thought about it, but as soon as I think about them at home waiting, I'm not comfortable going out and having fun by myself.

A: Wouldn't it be possible for everyone to go out together?

B: My parents don't like too many activities, and what's more, they think going out wastes a lot of money, which they are not used to.

A: Sometimes spending a little money to go out and have fun, and enjoying the weekend is worth it.

B: That is true. However, they still think that it's not worth spending money like this.

A: Old people and young people's way of thinking is just too different, this must be the generation gap between them?

B: Maybe it is.

A: Then you're just going to hang out at home?

B: At home, I love to listen to my father tell stories about his past experiences. I believe that by staying with them over the weekend, I am often able to learn many things that I can't learn from books, it is really worthwhile.

(Sunday, at home)

Daughter: Mom, are you washing clothes again? Let me do it.

Mom: I'm almost done. You go to eat some fruits. I knew you would be coming back, so I already prepared it for you.

Daughter: Why don't you use the washing machine?

Mom: Just a few pieces. There's no point in using the washing machine. It's a waste of electricity and water.

Daughter: Then what's the use in buying a washing machine?

Mom: I'm used to washing with my hands, and washing a few pieces of laundry is a little bit of physical exercise for me.

Daughter: Ok, then, I can only do it your way, but you had better not tire yourself out, otherwise, you're going to have to do it my way.

(Monday, before working)

Worker A: How did you spend your weekend?

Worker B: Saturday I went home to see the parents with my wife and child, and Sunday three of us went out to play.

Worker A: Sounds like the weekend went pretty well. Where did you go for fun?

Worker B: We went to the zoo in the morning, and then in the afternoon we went strolling in a shopping center nearby.

(A young person says)

Now we have two days for rest every week, the weekend is longer than before, and life is a lot richer. How to spend the weekend? Everyone is different. Some people like to get together with the whole family where everybody makes delicious food and talks about the news of the last week. Some people like to go out for a good time, climb mountains, go fishing, or whatever. Young people are busy dating at the weekends. For the sake of raising kids, some parents take their children to various kinds of supplementary classes to study. As for me, I like to go out to see exhibitions on Saturdays. I like to see all kind of art works, no matter they are classical or modern. After being busy a whole day, I can blissfully sleep late on Sundays, and get up whenever I want.

Lesson Nine   What Is the Real Gender Equality?

(At home)

Husband: Dear, how come you're home so late too? I'll help you make dinner.

Wife: It's not so late. I went upstairs at Mr. Zhang's for a while. They were arguing again.

Husband: Why were they arguing again?

Wife: It was because as soon as Mr. Zhang gets home, he just reclines the couch watching TV and smoking. When his wife come back home, she cleans the vegetables and makes dinner, but Mr. Zhang doesn't help her at all.

Husband: He shouldn't do like that! When two people work all day, they're both very tired. And when they get home, how can they not do anything but just let another do it all?

Wife: Exactly. She asks him to help cook dinner together, but he doesn't, and as a result, it makes her so mad that she cries.

Husband: How are the two of them now?

Wife: I told him that men and women should be equal in society and also in the family, and I told him a little bit about our experiences.

Husband: You didn't praise your model husband to them, did you?

Wife: It was because I praised you that Mr. Zhang changed his attitude and admitted his mistake to her, and the two of them happily made dinner together then.

Husband: I hope that today they will not fight over doing household chores. You did a good job mediating. But, you didn't tell them about how I acted when we first got married, did you?

Wife: I didn't talk about that, where do you think of the experience coming from?

Husband: How embarrassing! Our secret is no more safe.

(Elder sister and younger brother are chatting)

Brother: Sister, next week we have to put on a speech competition, can you help me to think of something to talk about?

Sister: Have you decided on a topic yet?

Brother: "Gender Equality."

Sister: Such a complex problem! There's too much to talk about, it won't be easy to organize. You have a hard time.

Brother: So, that's why I'm asking you to help me think. I don't know where I should start.

Sister: There are people talking about sexual equality all over the place. It's talked about in the newspapers, and they also talk about it on TV; they keep talking about it but even the simplest problem hasn't been cleared up.

Brother: What problem?

Sister: Now people generally think women can do anything men can do and it seems that we've already realized sexual equality.

Brother: What do you think?

Sister: Men have their own special characteristics and women have their own one too, you can't just start discussing from one point, that would be too simple.

(Younger brother is giving a speech)

"Gender equality" is always a hot topic in society. Equality is a political problem and an economic problem, it is also an ideology one. In the modern society, women and men similarly leave home to go to work, and this has set the political and economic foundation for sexual equality. But at present, the phenomena of "Gender inequality" in the society and families still exist. For instance, one way to put it is: "working well is not as good as marrying well for a woman". What does it take for a woman to be considered to have properly managed the relationship between her family and her career? How to reach real Gender equality?

Lesson Ten   I've Come Here Looking for Work

(On the phone)

Li Lin: Hello? Could you help me to ask Liu Shan to pick up the phone, please?

Office Worker:	Liu Shan? He hasn't been here for a long time!
Li Lin:	What? Where did he go?
Office Worker:	He has run a computer company and has become a boss now!
Li Lin:	Oh, What a surprise! Do you know how to get in touch with him?
Office Worker:	I'll give you his mobile phone number. He left it when he left.
Li Lin:	Hang on a second; I'll look for a piece of paper and a pencil. OK, go ahead.
Office Worker:	...did you write it down?
Li Lin:	Yes, thanks!

(In the manager's office of a computer company)

Li Lin:	Excuse me, Is manager Wang here?
Secretary:	What is this regarding? I'm his secretary.
Li Lin:	Hi, I've come looking for work. I saw the recruitment advertisement in the paper for your company, so...
Secretary:	Oh, Mr. Wang is out with a visitor right now. Can I have your resume first?
Li Lin:	OK. Do you think this resume is enough?
Secretary:	Do you have identification for your education?
Li Lin:	Yes, This is a copy of my diploma.
Secretary:	OK, I'll give it to him as soon as he gets back. As to the time of the interview, please wait for our phone call.

(The leaders of the company are on the interview)

A:	Why do you want to do this job?
Li:	I am very interestied in this kind of work.
B:	There are many computer companies, why do you want to come here?
Li:	You are "startup" company and have developed fast. I believe there is great potential for me to work here.
C:	What do you mean "potential"?
Zhang:	I mean I could improve my working ability and skills through working here. Of course it can also increase my income.
B:	Working here is very busy and you may not have a break during the weekend.
Li:	I'm young. I like the tough life. My mother always says: "Busy is happy." I think she is right.
A:	OK, your interview is over, please wait for us to inform you.

(A company manager says)

We recruit a group of new workers here every year. Among them, those middle aged workers impressed me most. As they are older and have a lot of experience. They have the technical skills, they become familiar with the work very fast as well. Additionally they are serious and responsible with their work, and I have confidence in them. Of course, many university graduates have come for interviews, a few of them have also become our new employees. They are enthusiastic, love to learn, and their technical skills and abilities have rapidly improved. We are very satisfied with them.

Lesson Eleven   We'd Like You to Attend Our Wedding

(Two colleagues are in the office)

A:	Hey, whose wedding candy?
B:	Secretary Li's.
A:	Did he get married? When was the ceremony performed?
B:	Yes, he got married, but they just had a meal with relatives and then he took his bride on a trip.
A:	No wonder he didn't come to work for the past few days. It turns out that he has become a groom. How long did they go?
B:	They need at least a week, I think.
A:	A travelling wedding, that's not bad.

B: What do you think? In the future you can also have a travelling wedding, OK?

A: I've got something even better.

B: What's more romantic?

A: That is a secret. I can't tell you right now.

(A couple goes to Wang Ping's home)

Young Man: Hello, Wang Ping!

Wang Ping: It's you. Please sit down! Oh, ... so, when are we going to eat your wedding candy?

Young Woman: June 16th. Saturday. We'd like you to attend our wedding.

Wang Ping: That is great. A good day, chosen well! Double six are double lucky! I'll definitely go! Prepare more wine for wedding!

(At the wedding banquet)

Master of Ceremonies: Now we'll all have a toast to the new bride and groom!

Guests: Cheers!

Master of Ceremonies: OK, now the wine has been drunk, the parents have been honored, what should we do?

Guest: The newlyweds should tell us their love story.

Groom: Don't embarrass us.

Master of Ceremonies: What day is today? They don't want to tell us, is it Ok?

Guests: No!

Groom: Oh, I'll go first.

Master of Ceremonies: OK, if he doesn't tell the whole story, bride can make additional statement.

Groom: We were classmates; at that time we didn't really know each other. Then one day after class, it was raining suddenly...

A Guest: That's really romantic!

A Guest: Be quiet and listen!

...

Master of Ceremonies: OK, everybody, what do you think their story?

A Guest: Great!

A Guest: Magnificent!

Master of Ceremonies: Come on, let's lift our glasses and wish the newlywed peace and harmony!

A Guest: And happy ever after.

(The master of ceremonies says)

I have been in charge of wedding ceremonies for over hundred newlyweds. The parents of the young couple today are my colleagues, so I am familiar with the two of them. The boy is intelligent, capable and good looking. The girl is smart and pretty; she is very knowledgeable and has broad interests. They love each other indeed and are really born for each other. To tell you the truth, I do envy them. I felt very happy to hold this ceremony for them. The best wishes to them together in the future!

(A TV host says)

We have been told recently, 51% of the people from Shanghai, Beijing and Guangzhou believe in the importance of "Holding a ceremony when getting married". Among them, 63% believe that "the location of the wedding ceremony is very important". 39% choose to have a wedding in a big hotel. 50% indicate "in order to remember this happiness forever, we would like to choose a good meaningful day to get married". This shows that contemporary people think very highly of marriage.

Lesson Twelve   People Who Love Life Will Be Young Forever

(In a teahouse, foreign students are chatting with Chinese students)

Foreigners: What do Chinese people usually do in the evening?

Chinese people:	People are different. Take me for example, I watch TV for most of time. Often there are some good dramas on TV during the evening, an episode a day, and one drama will have ten to twenty episodes, some have forty or fifty.
Foreigner:	So long!
Chinese:	If it's good it won't seem long.
Foreigner:	Except watching TV, what else to do?
Chinese:	Of those retired, some play cards, and some play mahjong. People who have jobs, like my sister as a teacher, she usually needs to do things like prepare for class, playing with her kids for a while, or doing household chores , etc., and then it's time for bed.
Foreigner:	And other young people?
Chinese:	They like to do things such as going out for a stroll, go dancing, or go to sing karaoke or something. Some of them go online and chat. And you?
Foreigner:	After a meal I like to go out for a walk, and then go back to my room and review what we have learned in the day-time; sometimes I make phone calls home, or surf the Internet and send E-mails.

(Two music fans are chating)

A:	Come on, listen, the song I've downloaded just sounds so good.
B:	Let me see it. How come I don't think it sounds good? I am old.
A:	Don't say that. You're only two years older than me. Could it be that you don't like popular music?
B:	I don't like it that much; more importantly I don't listen to it often. I still like old songs. The old songs of the past are really enjoyable.
A:	I've discovered that although we both are "music fans", there are many different kinds of fans. You like to watch classic movies and listen to old songs. But why didn't I have interest in those things?
B:	There's nothing strange about that, everyone has his or her own hobbies. But we do have something that we share in common. We all love music or we could say we are both music fans. Right?

(A middle-aged person says)

After working, I'm either in the kitchen or in my study. I've got two hobbies, one active—cooking, and one inactive—reading. Cooking is good for health; reading can exercise my mind. What do you think? Pretty scientific, huh? Do you think I should go out and get some sunshine? There's no need, just sitting on the balcony at my house I can enjoy the sunshine. And reading there is really cosy.

(A retired old man says)

My life is so interesting, every day I'm very happy. When I was young, I loved sports and played basketball, volleyball and tabletennis often. I love travelling. I've gone to a lot of places, visited many scenic spots and historical sites. I've also had a lot of jobs; I've been a teacher, a tour guide, and a lawyer. Although I'm retired already, I still have things I haven't done. See, I often go to a Senior Citizens Activity Center where retired people in community can be active and have fun together. It does seem that everyone becomes younger. That's why it's a known fact that people who love life will be young forever.

Lesson Thirteen   I'm a Person with a Gourmet's Luck

(At home)

Wife:	We've just moved into our new house. Why don't we invite our friends to get together and have a meal here?
Husband:	Sure, why not? I suggest we have a buffet.
Wife:	We can prepare some cold dishes, and cook more hot dishes. Whatever people like to eat, they can help themselves. Do we need wine?
Husband:	Of course we do. Other than beer, also order some wine and stuff.
Wife:	What about has some liquor?
Husband:	I don't think so, it is too strong. It is easy to get drunk by drinking liquor.

(At dinner table)

Host:	Why don't you eat?
Guests A:	I got up so late and not hungry yet.
Host:	You are not on a diet, are you?
Guests A:	Don't laugh at me. I'm getting fatter and have gained another few kilograms in the past months.
Guests B:	Who can say you are fat? You have such a nice figure.
Guest A:	I really admire you. No matter what you eat, you never get fat. You have gourmet's luck.
Guest C:	I think that health is more important than anything. Fat or thin, it's all what other people see, having good health, and feeling comfortable are the best.
Host:	Don't worry about eating, if you starve yourself then you will look sick. If you really want to be thinner, the best way is to do exercises.
Guest A:	I know it, but it's hard to stay active every day. As soon as you stop, you get fat.

(An American was invited to a Chinese home)

Host:	Are the eating habits very different between China and United States?
American:	Oh yeah, very much. I really like Chinese food, but I'm still not used to some habits.
Hostess:	For instance...
American:	When we have wine, the host is too enthusiastic, always making me drink, I'm often to embarrassed to say no, and sometimes drinking too much.
Host:	Actually at that time, all you need to do is to tell them that you don't drink, then they won't force you to drink. Everyone just do as you please.
Hostess:	If I were you, I would say: "Thanks, but I don't drink" or "I can only have a little".
American:	OK, I'll try it later.
Host:	I've been in the States. I'm not used to using knives and forks when eating. The left hand holds the fork, and the right hand holds the knife, you cut the meat and vegetable, it really bothers me. It is especially difficult when eating chicken, fish and noodles.
American:	It is the same as our westerners not being used to using chopsticks , it's not good if you don't have any practice.
Hostess:	The way you eat breakfast is also a little bit different from us. For example, you like to eat bread and to drink cold milk just out of the refrigerator, and you also drink fruit juice. My stomach can't just stand it. I like to drink hot soymilk, eat a fried pancake, and have a boiled egg.

(A foreigner says)

I am a lucky person, I find almost all foods delicious. I mean everything is delicious for me. I can eat anything, spicy, sweet, sour, and salty, it doesn't matter. It feels really good to try dishes from different areas. As I'm living in China, I don't want to go to McDonald's or Kentucky Fried Chicken because I should eat more Chinese food. This has been a great help to me in understanding China. Only when I'm homesick, I go and eat western food.

Lesson Fourteen   City or Countryside, Which is Favorable?

(At home)

Son:	We should also raise a pet at home. Would raising a puppy be good?
Daughter:	A puppy is lovely! I want to have one.
Mother:	A puppy is lovely but I disagree on raising one. It's too much trouble to raise a puppy in the city.
Son:	If we can't have a puppy, how about have a cat?
Daughter:	Yes, I want to have a white cat with the blue eyes. I will bathe it everyday.
Son:	And I will feed it everyday. Mom, you are not disagreeing, are you?
Mother:	I would ask for your dad's suggestion.

(In a real estate office, a manager is answering the questions)

Manager:	Would you like to buy a suburban house?
Client:	I just want to check the new houses here.
Manager:	Yes, please come over and see it. There are sets of two rooms and three rooms.
Client:	How many bathrooms in the set of three?
Manager:	There are two types, one bathroom and two bathrooms.
Client:	How about the sitting room? Isn't big?
Manager:	Quite big.
Client:	This place is located between the city and countryside. It's a good environment. What about transportation?
Manager:	There are quite a lot of public transportation routes here.
Client:	Is that convenient for going to school?
Manager:	You can see here, that is a middle school and this is a primary school. They are all close to each other.
Client:	What about a price?
Manager:	It's cheaper than houses downtown by about one third. Would you like to purchase one?
Client:	I need to make a decision after discussing it with my family first.

(At home)

Old brother:	I really don't understand. Other people are all thinking of ways of moving to the city, but you would rather move to the countryside. What's really going on here?
Younger brother:	I like the countryside life. I like nature and the simple peasants there. Our hometown has a wonderful surrounding, fresh air, the blue sky and the green hills. Cows and sheep are on the meadow eating grass, and it's like a painting, it's hard to describe how beautiful it is.
Old brother:	But how can living conditions in the countryside compare with those in the city? There are many things that are inconvenient in the countryside.
Younger brother:	That was before. There were hardships of living and working in countryside. But now things are changing a lot. If you don't believe me, go to the countryside and see for yourself. The life won't necessarily be worse than in the city. What's more, the pollution in the city from industry and transportations is getting worse and worse. It is nothing good for health at all.

(Younger brother says)

Is the city better or is the countryside better? This is something that can't be clarified in one sentence. There are too many people in the cities and the city is too crowdy. Where could be more comfortable than the countryside? Honestly, when I first came to the countryside, I thought I'll never get used to this and that was really inconvenient. But Economy is developing, society is making progress and agriculture is getting better. The peasants are richer now. There is less difference between the city and countryside day by day. The longer I live here, the deeper my feelings for the countryside.

Lesson fifteen   I'm Really Happy for You

(On the campus)

Chen Hong:	Wang Li, I heard you are going abroad to study?
Wang Li:	Nothing tangible is in sight yet. I just applied for it.
Chen Hong:	What sort of paperwork do you need to study abroad?
Wang Li:	First I've got to take an English test, something like the TOEFL, GRE and IELTS. If my scores are good, then I can apply for a scholarship.
Chen Hong:	You won't have any problems with the English. Doesn't everyone call you "a living dictionary"? It's almost no word you don't know.
Wang Li:	Who says? I didn't take IELTS, but took the TOFEL and GRE this time. I haven't gotten any scores yet.
Chen Hong:	If a school accepts you, the paperwork should be easier, huh?
Wang Li:	I'm not sure. All I know is that it takes a bunch of working days to get your passport, and to get a visa, an interview

is required among other things.

(At Wang Li's home)

Chen Hong:	The announcement letter from the school has arrived!
Wang Li:	Really? Quick, give it to me. Let me see.
Chen Hong:	What does it say on the top?
Wang Li:	Ah, it's a full scholarship!
Chen Hong:	When do you start school?
Wang Li:	August 26th.
Chen Hong:	How do you arrange your living?
Wang Li:	The school has a dorm, but you can also rent a house outside by yourself. The first year, however, the foreign students need to stay with a host family in order to improve their language more quickly.
Chen Hong:	That makes sense. Wang Li, congratulations, I'm really happy for you.
Wang Li:	Thanks! It was you who brought me good luck. I can only thank you!

(Wang Li says)

I have already arrived in America, becoming a graduate student. When doing the paperwork, I had so many problems. Now, I'm going to tell you about my experiences: To apply to become a graduate student in America, you must have an undergraduate mean score of eighty and above, also a score of eighty or above is required on the TOFEL ,6.5 or above is required on the IELTS exam. To apply for a scholarship, generally speaking a GRE score is required. In addition, you must submit a letter of recommendation, a published thesis, research findings, proof of field experience, etc.

(Chen Hong says)

There is a saying that: Everyone has his or her own ideals. I'm really happy for Wang Li to study abroad. She is one of the thousands of Chinese who go abroad to work or study. Then honestly, I don't want to go abroad. There are many reasons, for instance, who will take care of my mother if I go abroad? Also, my major is much more suitable for study in the country. Domestic conditions are getting better and better, there are more and more good academic advisors, you can also succeed by studying domestically.

Lesson Sixteen   A Toast to Friendship!

(Students at a farewell party)

A:	How could you just come? The party has begun for a while.
B:	Sorry, I mistook the time and had you waiting for a long time.
C:	Fine him a glass of wine!
B:	I don't like beer anyhow, give me a glass of wine.
D:	OK, everybody is here. Now let me propose a toast. First, to all of us becoming good friends in China. Cheers!
B:	And wish to see each other again.Cheers!
C:	The time really flies! The years of foreign student's life has passed just like that.
D:	Yeah, it's really fast. The scene of when we first entered the school seems just like yesterday.
A:	Do you still remember how we looked when we first met, you were wearing a yellow jacket, he was wearing a gray sweater, and she had really long, straight hair...
B:	Then you could never tell us apart, and you often called us by the wrong name.
A:	What about you? Always answering wrong questions in class and making a joke?
D:	Later on he became a model student. He can speak Chinese as fluently as a Chinese now.
B:	No, no, it's not enough and there is a long way to go.
D:	I suggest that everyone here uses the language of his or her own country to say "a toast to friendship"!
A:	An interesting proposal. OK, one, two, three!

| Students: | A toast to friendship! |
| D: | One more suggestion. How about taking a picture for all of us? |

(In the dorm)

Jin Yunfu:	Peter, have you packed everything?
Peter:	Pretty much. It's a little unbearable when it comes the time to leave. After we are apart, I don't know when we'll be able to see each other again.
Jin Yunfu:	Don't be sad. I believe that we'll definitely have the opportunity to meet again later on. What time is your flight?
Peter:	Twelve o'clock. I need to get to the airport two hours beforehand.
Jin Yunfu:	Is anyone seeing you off?
Peter:	Yeah, they said they will go downstairs together.
Jin Yunfu:	Oh, it's nine o'clock. It's time to go down.
Peter:	It must be. Good-bye, my room! Good-bye, my bed!
Jin Yunfu:	Let me help you carry your luggage, I'll see you to the cab.

(Friends see Peter off at the airport)

A:	The plane is about to take off. Quick, get on board.
Peter:	I really hate to leave you guys. Don't forget me.
B:	How can we? Write us when you can.
Peter:	If you have the chance to come to my country, contact me for sure.
C:	Don't forget to send us a wedding picture of you and your wife when you get married.
Peter:	Hey, I'll remember.
D:	Have a good trip!
A:	Please say hello to your parents.
Peter:	Thanks! Good-bye!
Groups:	Good-bye!

(Peter says)

My sojoum as a foreign student in China is over. I'm both happy and sad. I'm happy that I was able to learn real Chinese, make a lot of friends, go to a lot of scenic places and historic sites, understand more of China's past and present. What's sad is that I really hate to leave China; I hate to leave my school, my teachers, and classmates. I have a wish: when I get home, I will continue improving my Chinese, pay attention to the situations in China, In this way get a wider understanding of China.